Rain Right

NOW,

Lord!

HOW TO GET YOUR CUP
SO FULL OF JESUS
THAT NOTHING ELSE CAN FIT.

FROM DOUG PERRY

www.FellowshipOfTheMartyrs.com
fotm@fellowshipofthemartyrs.com

Copyright © 2006 Doug Perry, Fellowship Of The Martyrs

ISBN: 1463794436
ISBN-13: 978-1463794439

FELLOWSHIP
OF THE
MARTYRS

The Bride gets her jewelry, but it's going to hurt to get it on,
and once you're used to it, you're never going to want to
rip it back off again. Heaven is free. HOLINESS is hard!
If not us, who? If not here, where? If not now, when?

DEDICATION

This book is dedicated to Jesus Christ.
In fact, everything I've written, recorded, sung,
spoken or ever done is dedicated to Jesus Christ.
Not that it was all perfect, but that's not His fault.
If you don't like it, blame me, not Him.

I want to take special note of the people who were so
instrumental in helping grow me. Some were used to
encourage me, some were used to teach me patience, some
were used by God to motivate me to find the demon on them
that I might never have seen if they weren't on my last nerve.
Some taught me to endure persecution, even from the closest
friend. Some showed me holiness. Praise God! They were all a
blessing and I really do love them all. (You know which one
you were.)

Bob, Nancy, David, Marilyn, Kim, Constance, Stephanie, Ric, Brad, Keith, Steve,
Minnie, Jeannie and Stevie, Andrew, Rachael, Elijah, Bob, Clare, Gary, Kristi, James,
Cindy, Helen, Sherri, Jen, Dennis, Merri, Joseph, Gary, Cary, Emily, Lili, David,
Yolanda, Suzanne, Tabitha, Josh, Austin, Chris, Candi, Nataliya, Helen, Ron, Rusty,
Josh, Barry, Barron, Glynda, Steve, Bianca, June, Andrew, John, Lisa, Diane, Larry,
Dewey, Jason, Sarah, Dave, Doug, Michael, Nichole, Dorothy, Tyler, Ky, Kathy,
Lizzie, Patrick, Sharon, Stevean, Randy, Bob, Casey, Amy, Cathy, Chuckie, Roger,
Nils, Ryan, Shelly, Kurt, Sharon, John, Mikey, Becky, James, Jennie, Angela, Gus,
Zach, Jason, Jacob, Greg, Tres, Daniel, J.R., Tatianna, Patti and Carolyn and
HUNDREDS that I pray will not feel left out but I don't have room to mention.

And a couple million intercessors all over the world pouring
their hearts out and crying rivers on our behalf without whom
I'm not sure how we could have made it
this far. I'm humbled. Please don't stop praying.

I love you all and I'm not going to stop no matter what.

CONTENTS

ACKNOWLEDGMENTS

This book really should not be read all on its own.
It is a part of a larger understanding, a series of books written about what is wrong with "church." The statistics are covered in the book, "*The Apology To The World.*" The book, "*The Red Dragon: the horrifying truth about why the 'church' cannot seem to change*" extends on this and shows the supernatural roots and the solution to wipe the slate clean and reboot. The book, "*Do It Yourself City Church Restoration*" lays the foundation scripturally for what Church should look like and how we rebuild this. And the book, "*DEMONS?! You're kidding right?*" shows how it's under attack and how to defend it. Before we can fix a system, we have to fix each individual, so for personal tune-ups, the book, "*Dialogues with God*" is helpful to learn to hear God better and "*Who Neutered The Holy Spirit?!*" is for those who think God isn't as supernatural as He used to be.

God has been pouring out a lot on Liberty, Missouri.
We continue to pray and believe that this will be a refuge, a haven, a training and equipping center.
If you're looking for a different kind of "church," something more real and more life-changing, and if the Lord leads, you're welcome in Liberty. When (not if) things hit the fan, if you can make it here, we'll do our best to love you and make a way through all that is coming together.

www.FellowshipOfTheMartyrs.com
fotm@fellowshipofthemartyrs.com

*"Your growth in Christ
is directly proportional
to your willingness
to RUSH HEADLONG
into the refining fire
and give it a wet, sloppy kiss."*

- Doug Perry

SPIRITUAL GIFTS –
HOW TO GET THEM AND
WHY YOU SHOULD SHARE THEM.

Romans 12:6-8 (Amplified)
Having then gifts differing according to the grace that is given to us, whether prophecy, [let us prophesy] according to the proportion of faith; Or ministry, [let us wait] on [our] ministering: or he that teacheth, on teaching; Or he that exhorteth, on exhortation: he that giveth, [let him do it] with simplicity; he that ruleth, with diligence; he that sheweth mercy, with cheerfulness.

I Corinthians 12:10-11 (Amplified)
10 To another the working of miracles, to another prophetic insight (the gift of interpreting the divine will and purpose); to another the ability to discern and distinguish between [the utterances of true] spirits [and false ones], to another various kinds of [unknown] tongues, to another the ability to interpret [such] tongues. 11 All these [gifts, achievements, abilities] are inspired and brought to pass by one and the same [Holy] Spirit, Who apportions to each person individually [exactly] as He chooses.

I Corinthians 12:28 (Amplified)
So God has appointed some in the church [for His own use]: first apostles; second prophets; third teachers; then wonder-workers; then those with ability to heal the sick; helpers; administrators; [speakers in] different (unknown) tongues.

Let's start with some qualifying questions just to save everybody some time here:

1. **Do you think the Gifts of the Spirit are all still active and for today?**
   Yes – Proceed to Page 5
   No – See next question.

2. **Would you LIKE for them to be for today, but you just aren't sure?**
   Yes – See next question
   No – How exactly do you plan to fulfill Mark 16:15-20 without them? Do you realize that you're in the minority now? The growth in the Church worldwide is nearly all people that disagree with you. You are directly insulting the personal experience of about 800 million Christians – at least some of whom are NOT tools of satan and filled with demons! You have to come to the conclusion that every tongue, every miracle, every healing, all the people that were raised from the dead in the last 1900 years is all bogus and from satan. It just ain't so! God doesn't change.

   Miracles are happening all over the world and you can't blame them all on satan! I was where you are, I know what you're thinking, but you gotta look around and see that God is moving. This stuff is real and you're powerless against the badness if you're not so FULL of Jesus that nothing else can fit. Please take God out of the box you put Him in and let Him be God. He doesn't change. His promises are always the same. He's still does cool stuff. If you can't believe He's big enough to still act like He used to, you might be better off to not read any further.

3. Do you think SOME of the Gifts are for today, but not all of them?

Yes – Close enough. Go to Page 5

No – OK, so we don't have Wisdom anymore? Giving? Administration? Faith? Hospitality? So when the Bible was done being written that which was perfect was come so that which was in part was done away? Is that the argument you're going to stick with? So how come some ended but others didn't? Who gets to pick and choose? God changes, but only partially? This argument is indefensible. Either they all ended or none of them did. You can't pick and choose. And if they all ended, then how come the enemy still has all his weapons? How come they have spells and curses and zombies and astral projection and psychics and mediums? If "that which is perfect" came, then why isn't evil completely vanquished? Where are our cool toys?! Is "that which is perfect" how we got 41,000+ denominations?

I love you. I really do, but you're just flat wrong and you're insulting a whole lot of people at the same time. You're saying God changes and He doesn't talk to us anymore and do big stuff and I just happen to know you're really, really wrong. It would be great if you would go ahead and read this book, but you're probably just going to argue with everything and close your mind, so it's probably better stewardship of your time if you just stop reading now.

If I'm right, then God is about to burst onto the scene in a great big giant way and you will have a really, REALLY hard time sustaining your argument that He doesn't do that stuff anymore. In fact, you're probably going to have to repent a LOT to Him and to anybody you led astray. But it's His job to fix you, so I'll just leave it to Him. In the meantime, get online and Google "Iris Ministries", "John G. Lake", "Smith Wigglesworth" or "Brother Yun" and see which ones you think are the biggest liars and tools of Satan. I dare you.

Still here? Great!!

This is going to change your life!

Let's get started.

Questions

IF there is a war between good and evil,
THEN the Gifts of the Spirit are offensive and
defensive weapons.

IF the Gifts of the Spirit are fixed and predetermined and
unchangeable,
THEN how can we adjust to a changing battlefield?

IF people only get one Gift each,
THEN why are we told to desire more and greater Gifts?

IF nobody can have ALL the Gifts,
THEN why do we have examples of people that did/do?

IF we specifically DENY some of the Gifts,
THEN who benefits most – God or satan?

IF we assert that certain Gifts aren't for today,
THEN aren't we operating with less than complete
weaponry systems?

IF we acknowledge the validity of certain Gifts
but ban them from our assemblies,
THEN aren't we violating specific commands
not to do that (and being rude to the Gift Giver)?

IF we acknowledge the validity of all the Gifts,
but we're missing some of them in our assembly,
THEN shouldn't we get somebody with the missing
pieces or seek it until God gives it to us?

Ephesians 6:12 – *For our struggle is not against flesh and blood, but against the rulers, against the authorities, against the powers of this dark world and against the spiritual forces of evil in the heavenly realms.*

I Corinthians 12:31a – *But eagerly desire the greater gifts.*
I Corinthians 7:7 – *For I would that all men were even as I myself. But every man hath his proper gift of God, one after this manner, and another after that.*

I Corinthians 14:1 – *Follow the way of love and eagerly desire spiritual gifts, especially the gift of prophecy.*

I Corinthians 14:12 – *So it is with you. Since you are eager to have spiritual gifts, try to excel in gifts that build up the church.*

I Corinthians 14:39-40 – *Therefore, my brothers, be eager to prophesy, and do not forbid speaking in tongues. 40 But everything should be done in a fitting and orderly way.*

<u>Assertions</u>

IF there is a war between good and evil,
THEN I want to be on the side of good.

IF evil seems to be winning,
THEN maybe we're not equipped fully.

IF there are weapons or armor that God has for me,
THEN I want them!

IF I pray to be like Jesus, **THEN** I probably need all available offensive and defensive weaponry systems.

IF there are varying levels of strength within each system,
THEN I want mine dialed all the way up!

IF getting more of Him requires less of Me,
THEN I'm all for it! Crucify me daily. Kill it all.

IF Jesus says, "Ask and it shall be given,"
THEN why not ask for them all?

Ephesians 6:12 – *For our struggle is not against flesh and blood, but against the rulers, against the authorities, against the powers of this dark world and against the spiritual forces of evil in the heavenly realms.*

I Corinthians 12:31a – *But earnestly desire and zealously cultivate the greatest and best gifts and graces (the higher gifts and the choicest graces).* (Amplified)

Luke 11:13 – *If you then, though you are evil, know how to give good gifts to your children, how much more will your Father in heaven give the Holy Spirit to those who ask him!"*

Romans 8:32 – *He that spared not his own Son, but delivered him up for us all, how shall he not with him also freely give us all things?*

Why don't more people have all the Gifts? If you don't have, it's because you don't ask. (Or He knows you're going to make it about YOU instead of about JESUS.) What if more people don't have more Gifts because we're not sharing like we should?

IF God asks us to be a steward of some gift,
THEN we should invest it and get a return.

IF we bury it in the sand or don't use it, **THEN** we will be lukewarm and stagnant and He will spew us out.

IF we can share our Gifts of the Spirit with others,
THEN why aren't we?

We are three part beings – Body, Soul and Spirit. Who benefits most from fat, brainy, spiritually weak Christians?

Do we know how to feed the poor in spirit? Do we know how to pour ourselves out spiritually? Is there even such a thing? What can we pour out on them? How do we do it? Are we supposed to?

Yep. You're supposed to take the Gifts that you were given and invest them into other people. You're supposed to take all the Jesus in your "cup" and pour it out onto others. Just as you would with physical resources, you're supposed to spend your spiritual resources on others. As the Charisma of the Holy Spirit was poured out onto us, so we should pour it out on one another.

Can I prove it? You betcha! I'm not just spouting off here, God showed me where to look to prove it.

The word used in the Greek to refer to the Gifts of the Spirit is "charisma." (Hence, those who believe the gifts are real and for today are called "Charismatics.") It is basically simply the Holy Spirit, but from His presence comes multiple "weapons systems". This verse below says that we are to equip each other for this war by **sharing the spiritual gifts that we have been given**. In fact, it's a command and it infers that if you don't, you're not a good steward.

> I Peter 4:10 - KJV
> As every man hath received the gift (charisma), even so minister (diakoneo) the same one to another, as good stewards of the manifold (poikilos) grace (charis) of God.

Charisma is Strong's number 5486 and is translated 17 times as "gift" or "free gift". And defined as follows:

1) a favour with which one receives without any merit of his own
2) the gift of divine grace
3) the gift of faith, knowledge, holiness, virtue
4) the economy of divine grace, by which the pardon of sin and eternal salvation is appointed to sinners in consideration of the merits of Christ laid hold of by faith
5) grace or gifts denoting extraordinary powers, distinguishing certain Christians and enabling them to serve the church of Christ, the reception of which is due to the power of divine grace operating on their souls by the Holy Spirit

Diakoneo is translated here as to "minister", but the Strong's definition is much richer:

1) to be a servant, attendant, domestic, **to serve**, wait upon
   a) to minister to one, render ministering offices to
      1) to be served, ministered unto
   b) to wait at a table and offer **food and drink** to the guests,
      1) of women preparing food
   c) to minister i.e. **supply food and necessities of life**
      1) to relieve one's necessities (e.g. by collecting alms), to provide take care of, **distribute**, the things necessary to **sustain life**
      2) to take care of the **poor and the sick**, who administer the office of a deacon
      3) in Christian churches to serve as deacons
   d) to minister
      1) **to attend to anything, that may serve another's interests**
      2) **to minister a thing to one, to serve one or by supplying any thing**

Poikilos is translated here "manifold" but defined by Strong's as:

1) a various colours, variegated
2) of various sorts

It is translated eight times as "divers" and twice as "manifold".

The charisma isn't one "flavor." The Holy Spirit is a rainbow and when He is in us, He can manifest in a whole bunch of different ways. As with a prism, the amount of light that can come through is simply a matter of how transparent it is. The more transparent we are, the more the Holy Spirit can be seen and used through us in all the different colors. If God has given us a particular color and somebody else needs it, we should share.

Charis is translated "grace" in this passage
  1) grace
    a) that which affords joy, pleasure, delight,
        sweetness, charm, loveliness: grace of speech.
  2) good will, loving-kindness, favour
    a) of the merciful kindness by which God, exerting
        his holy influence upon souls, turns them to Christ,
        keeps, strengthens, increases them in Christian
        faith, knowledge, affection, and kindles them to the
        exercise of the Christian virtues
  3) what is due to grace
    a) the spiritual condition of one governed by the
        power of divine grace
    b) the token or proof of grace, benefit
      1) a gift of grace
      2) benefit, bounty
      4) thanks, (for benefits, services, favours),
          recompense, reward

Ok, I'm sure you're already thinking that I'm interpreting that verse incorrectly. You probably looked up the NIV version of this verse and it says:

> I Peter 4:10 NIV – *Each one should use whatever gift he has received to serve others, faithfully administering God's grace in its various forms.*

Yeah, it does sound like you're just supposed to use your gift wisely to serve others, not "pour it out" on people. But try Young's Literal Translation:

> I Peter 4:10 YLT – *each, according as he received a gift, to one another ministering it, as good stewards of the manifold grace of God;*

How about Darby?

> I Peter 4:10 – *each according as he has received a gift, ministering it to one another, as good stewards of [the] various grace of God.*

Wow! I love this one! The Wycliffe New Testament:

> I Peter 4:10 – *each man as he hath received grace, ministering it into each other [ministering each to other], as good dispensers of the manifold grace of God.*

"Ministering it"? Don't they mean ministering WITH IT? Using it effectively? Well, that too, but I'm just pretty sure this verse means that you should steward the gift that was given to you **by giving it <u>into</u> other people** as the Lord directs. We are to all be "**good dispensers**" of the manifold, multi-faceted, variegated *charis* of God. Are you doing that?
Look at the King James again:

> I Peter 4:10 – *As every man hath received the gift* (charisma), *even so minister* (diakoneo) *the <u>same</u> one to another, as good stewards of the manifold* (poikilos) *grace* (charis) *of God.*

The same what? The same gift you just got. Distribute it to others. What else do you have to share except what's inside you? By giving it away, you'll get more. That's God's economy. People that say the "charisma" aren't for today say you can't lay hands on someone and have them receive the Holy Spirit, but that's exactly what this verse commands us to do – in all His flavors and colors. People that believe in the "charisma" will lay hands on people to transfer the Gift of Tongues, but they don't seem to get that the application is the same for ALL the various flavors. And it's not a one-time thing either. Whatever we have we should share. If we get something new, we should bring it to the Body and share. That's how everybody gets fully equipped.

We are to pour our Gifts out onto each other. We are to share all that we have with those in need. We are to empty our cup onto those around us. Anyone that hoards that which God has given and buries it in the ground will be punished severely and cast into the darkness where there will be weeping and gnashing of teeth. Read the Parable of the Talents – Matthew 24:14-30. How can it not apply? You have physical, emotional and spiritual assets. You should be sharing ALL of them.

Still not buying it? That you can pass out Gifts of the Spirit? Well, you can't exactly. God's not going to let you give something to somebody that's not ready for it or He doesn't want to have it. And it's not about YOU anyway. But you most definitely CAN be the vehicle that transfers the Gifts that He's given you to somebody else. Or you can at least be willing and try. Don't believe me? Want me to prove it? Good, that's very Berean of you.

How about these?

Romans 1:11 – *For I long to see you, that I may impart* (metadidomi) *unto you some spiritual gift* (charisma), *to the end ye may be established.*

Metadidomi is Strong's number 3330 – to impart or to give – and is used in scripture for both physical and spiritual assets. Paul's not talking about the Baptism of the Holy Spirit here because He's writing to the Church of Rome which is already established. He's talking about distributing to them gifts they don't already have. Sharing from His abundance with any that has a need. Paul's cup overflowed so he had plenty to share. He seemed to have all the gifts – and in large measure.

Here's another one:

I Thessalonians 2:8 – So being affectionately desirous of you, we were willing to have imparted (metadidomi) unto you, not the gospel of God only, but also our own souls (psuche), because ye were dear unto us.

They were willing to share EVERYTHING with the Thessalonians. All that they had, every spiritual resource.

Strong's 5590 is "psuche" and has these meanings:
1) breath
   a) the breath of life
      1) the vital force which animates the body and shows itself in breathing
         a) of animals
         b) of men
   b) life
   c) that in which there is life
      1) a living being, a living soul
      2) the soul
         a) the seat of the feelings, desires, affections, aversions (our heart, soul etc.)
         b) the (human) soul in so far as it is constituted that by the right use of the aids offered it by

God it can attain its highest end and secure eternal blessedness, the soul regarded as a moral being designed for everlasting life

c) the soul as an essence which differs from the body and is not dissolved by death (distinguished from other parts of the body)

In the King James it is translated as soul 58, life 40, mind 3, heart 1, heartily +1537 1, not translated 2; 105 occurrences.

It's clear that they were willing to pour all they had into the Thessalonians. Every gift, every breath, whatever good thing they had.

Need more?

I Timothy 4:14 – *Be not negligent of the gift* (charisma) [that is] *in thee, which has been given* (didomi) *to thee through prophecy, with imposition of the hands of the elderhood.* (Young's)

I Timothy 4:14 – *Do not neglect your gift* (charisma), *which was given* (didomi) *you through a prophetic message when the body of elders laid their hands on you.* (NIV)

Are they talking about his calling? A calling is not a "charisma." A calling is "klesis." Are they talking about his commissioning service as a missionary? That doesn't sound right either. Paul is exhorting him to not neglect a charisma that was GIVEN to him by the body of elders and a prophetic utterance. Is this one gift or more than one? Well, "charisma" is not singular, so we can't assume it's a single Gift – like healing or tongues – but rather a manifold, diverse gifting for service.

OK, so he got Gift(s) when the elders laid hands on him. Was Paul there? Or did He do it also?

2 Timothy 1:6 – *For this reason I remind you to kindle afresh* (anazopureo) *the gift of God which is in you through the laying on of my hands.* (NAS)

Anazopureo (Strong's 329) – means to kindle up, inflame one's mind, strength, zeal

Some versions say "stir up the gift" but what they literally mean is to stir as a fire. To get it flaming red hot again. To not let the light or the heat die out. If Paul told Timothy to stir it up, it must be that there were varying degrees of the same gift. That is, you could let it die down from lack of attention or use. Do you know how to "kindle afresh" the gift of God which is in you? Do you know for sure that you even have the gift of God in you?

I'm pretty sure that God's economy has a simple rule about how to multiply or increase what you have – you share it sacrificially with someone else. Then you get more – or what you have gets stronger. That's Kingdom Economics 101.

So do you think that in all the time that Paul spent with Timothy (who he considered a son), that he ever laid his hand on him and prayed that the Lord would give Timothy any good gift that God had ever given Paul? Don't you think that, whether or not Paul was with the elders in I Tim 4:14, that Paul also poured himself out into Timothy over and over during their time together? I know that I do with the people I love and fellowship with.

I want to pause here and say that this book isn't just about Spiritual Gifts, it's about how to be full of Jesus. He is the fullness of all the gifts, all the fruit, all the faith, hope and love. If you can be filled with Jesus, crammed full until nothing else can fit, then you will see more and more of the gifts show up – and more and more fruit of the Spirit. Besides being a Biblical imperative that you be FULL of the Spirit of God, it's really the only way to peace and joy and victory. This book is not about seeking manifestations, this is about being effectively armored and weaponed up for the war that we're fighting that TOO MANY people are asleep during. This book is about raising up the Church to walk in the fullness of all that Christ has for us. Not just healing and speaking in tongues, but wisdom and discernment and administration and prophecy and all the callings that are necessary for what's coming.

Before we can get too far into the talk about Spiritual Gifts, we need to first make sure that the fundamentals are covered, that everyone is free of the chains that bind them and the embedded sin that is keeping the fountain of living water inside of them from bursting forth. Before we can get your cup overflowing, we have to pull the cork out! Most of this book is about understanding the power that God has for you, the walk He desires for you, the promises He made you, the fear of the Lord that you need to have to keep this from being about YOU – and the expectation to LOVE that He places on you in exchange for the wondrous gifts He gives you.

My greatest hope is that through this you would just end up with a great, big, giant cup of Jesus and you'd learn how to keep your cup full all the time. If we can get you crammed full of Jesus, then He'll take care of the rest. You can't be full of Jesus without getting more gifts. That's really the point.

You getting it? Convinced yet?

**If you're still not buying it, then you
probably still don't even believe
the "charisma" are for today.**

**If that's true, you better stop reading,
'cause this is just going to get weirder and weirder.**

TRIPARTITE AXIOMS

Tripartite simply means "three part" and an axiom is just a logic progression to prove a point. So I've just strung a few together here to see if you can get the point of where we're going. I could write a whole 200 page paperback about this by telling lots of stories and fluffing it up, but there's a war between good and evil and we're kind of losing, so it's probably better if we just cut out all the fluff and get right to the point.

God is tripartite – Father, Son and Holy Spirit.
IF we were made in God's image,
THEN we are tripartite – Soul, Body and Spirit.

When God heals us, it affects all three.
When God asks for obedience, it means from all three.
When God asks for worship, it means from all three.

When we sin, it affects all three – Soul, Body and Spirit.
When we disobey, it affects all three – Soul, Body and Spirit.

When we set ourselves above God, it affects all three – Soul, Body and Spirit.

When we are commanded to bear each other's burdens, it means all three.

When we are commanded to lift the yokes of oppression, it means all three.

When we are commanded to feed the hungry, it means all three.

When we give food to the hungry we are feeding their Body.

When we give Godly instruction to the hungry we are feeding their mind and Soul.

When we give blessings and prayers to the hungry we are feeding their Spirit.

When we give drink to the thirsty we are satiating their Body.

When we give pure truth to the thirsty, we are feeding their mind and Soul.

When we pour out on them the Living Water in us, we are feeding their Spirit.

We are vessels of honor, committed to the service of God.

We contain all kinds of things that can be used for His purposes.

We hold strength, money, time, knowledge, experience, wisdom, faith, love, joy, peace, patience.

Some are physical, some are mental, some are spiritual. All are to be shared.

The easiest to understand and do is the Body.

Even the world is good at disaster relief and feeding the hungry.

Even the wicked love their children and feed them good things.

The sneaky one is the Soul and the Mind.

Satan always wants us to spend all our energies on that one.

Teach them, train them, argue about philosophies, speculate about hypotheticals.

That is the Tree of the Knowledge of Good and Evil.

The world is really good at writing books and speaking many words. Of that there is no end.

The rarest one, the realest one, the most impactful one is the Spirit.

Our battle is NOT against flesh and blood – or the mind – it's against spiritual rulers.

Spiritual rulers that try to steal, kill and destroy.

You can starve the Spirit by overfeeding the Body and Soul.

All you have to do is take all the emphasis away from the Spirit and put it on the Mind.

God instituted the five fold Ministry for a reason. Each has their unique role.

Pastors are for feeding the Body. Caring for widows and orphans.

Teachers are for feeding the Mind. Train them up in the way they should go.

Evangelists are for igniting the Spirit in man and turning it over to God.

Prophets identify the failings in the process individually or corporately and point them out loudly.

Apostles train them all up and set them into place and send them out - and are themselves sent out.

All should be fully pouring themselves out on behalf of those in need – Body, Soul and Spirit.

Do we know how to pour out the Spirit on someone in need?

Do we know how to make sure our own cup is full? Is anybody teaching that anymore?

Isn't it obvious that the Church in America's Body is well fed?

How many thousands of tons of potato salad do we serve at fellowship suppers every year?

How much do we weigh per capita? We have plenty of food.
Who could argue?
In fact, too much in some places and not enough in others, but
that's just a distribution problem.

Isn't it obvious that the Church in America's Mind is well fed?
Could we have any more books and tapes and conferences and
satellite training meetings?
Could our soulish nature be any more gratified? Do we not
have enough input?
We are more obese and overfed in the Mind than we are in the
Body.

> *"Repent of your sins, accept Jesus into your heart.*
> *There now. We're done with your Spirit.*
> *We'll focus on your Body and your Mind from now on."*

Is that really working?

Isn't it obvious that the Church in America is poor in Spirit and
starving to death?
We don't look like Jesus, because we don't have nearly enough
of Him living in us.
Our spiritual cups are too small.
We don't love like Jesus, because we don't know how to share
what we do have.
Our spiritual cups are stagnant and lukewarm.
We don't act like Jesus, because we're leaving out the most
important part of the battle.
We're fighting on the wrong fronts.

We are raising up very large people with very large brains.
We are not raising up people with faith like a child that will
stride out with five stones against Goliath.
We are not raising up people that know how to walk in the
Spirit and in the Power of God.

We are not fulfilling the Great Commission holistically – Body, Soul and Spirit.

We are not fulfilling Isaiah 58 holistically – Body, Soul and Spirit.

We don't know how to fight in the spirit.

We don't know how to pray anymore.

Not really. Not all night with travailing and crying out for God.

Not pulling down strongholds and lifting yokes of oppression over our town, our church or our sheep.

We are spiritual warfare pygmies.

Whose idea could that have been?

Who is glorified most by overweight, brainy, spiritually week Christians?

When are we going to start feeding their spirits?

When are we going to start pouring ourselves out?

When is the rain going to start falling on the Church?

When is God going to pour out His Spirit on all flesh?

MY EXPERIENCE WITH
THE HOLY SPIRIT

Most folks with any experience with the Holy Spirit at all in this way will see that if someone without the Gift of Tongues lays hands on someone that wants it, probably nothing will happen. You can't pour out what you don't have. I've been to dozens of different kinds of congregations in the last few years. I've prayed with all kinds of people. How come some congregations all seem to sound the same when they pray in the Spirit? Either they're all faking it or something else is going on. Maybe the same pastor prayed on most of them and they all got what he's got. He poured out HIS Gift of Tongues on everybody he prayed for and so they all have the same "flavor" or "frequency" or "color". Can that really happen? Yep. I've seen it over and over.

Some time ago I was at a prayer meeting and a brother who has the gift of singing in the Spirit was there. It's really pretty! He'll get whole songs – music, lyrics and all – spontaneously from God. He can just sing for hours and sometimes in English and sometimes in another of several different languages. He'll sing a verse in a tongue and then interpret it himself into English without missing a beat. It's really worshipful and really pretty. Anyway, the Lord suggested to me that I ask him if he would give me that. Occasionally I would sing when I was praying, but it wasn't like what he does! He prayed about it and felt that the Lord said it was OK, so I just knelt down and he put his hand on my shoulder and asked the Lord to give me whatever he had. As I always do, I asked the Lord to keep me from getting anything other than what the Lord wanted for me and I just received it in faith.

A few days later when I finally had some quiet time alone, I was praying and just started singing. At first it was like a toddler's first steps and I was glad nobody was around, but then a real pretty little melody line came out and a verse in tongues, then the interpretation in English. Then another verse and another. It was a pretty and furiously harsh prophetic statement that was straight from God. I didn't have to think about it or create it or get things to rhyme in my head, it just came out. Then the Lord said to write it down. I was worried I would forget it all, but since it wasn't my brain, it was from the Spirit in me and He doesn't forget stuff, it was really easy. A couple of days later another song came. I look forward to practicing with what the Lord gave me and getting really good at it. If the Lord gives you a weapon, don't let it get rusty! Learn to be a sharpshooter!

Over and over I have prayed for people to receive my Gift of Discernment of Spirits and right away they start seeing in the spirit better. I've given away my Wisdom, my Peace, my Faith, my Prophecy, my Word of Knowledge, my Interpretation of Tongues, all of it. Whatever they needed as the Lord would lead and I've seen those people almost immediately begin to walk in those or be stronger in those than they were before. Sometimes dramatically so! Even people from denominations that don't believe in any of this stuff start hearing God better and having more dreams and knowing things ahead of time. It's really fun to watch!

How did I get all that stuff? Some of it God gave me Himself, but lots of if it came from other people that God sent to pray on me and equip me. One would come with lots of Discernment and pour herself into me. Another with Wisdom, another with Healing. Then the Lord showed me that the more you give it away, the more He'll give you. So I poured out whatever I had on people and God increased my portion. Sometimes I far exceeded the original person that came to pray for me because they didn't really see what they were doing and weren't actively and intentionally doing it all the time. God even sent people from other countries to my little furniture store to pray for me!

How did this crazy ride start? Well I was hungry for more of the Holy Spirit and none of my Baptist friends seem to know how to get more Holy Spirit in you. I didn't have peace and joy and victory and I knew God was calling me for something big and I didn't feel equipped. So I found some folks that seemed to believe you could actually get FULL of Jesus and they prayed with me. I didn't ask for tongues – it's at the bottom of the list – I asked for Wisdom in as big a measure as He could give me. In fact, I asked to see through the eyes of Jesus and told Him that any bit of me He wanted to kill so that Christ in me could live, He was welcome to it. I asked to be crammed so full of Jesus that nothing else could fit. I asked that the Lord would give me SO much of His Spirit that there wouldn't be ANY left for anybody else. I begged and pleaded and fully expected Him to give me a great big portion of His Spirit. And He did – and it instantly turned my life upside down! A whole bunch of stuff just burned out of me right on the spot and I started hearing Him better and having dreams and visions and praying all night and speaking other languages and people started coming to help and advise me. Radical people with BIG cups of Jesus. And they poured into me and grew me and the Lord had me start fasting all the time and that helped stretch me; and He tried me and tested me and refined me; and more and more persecution came, but I didn't care because I was so full of Jesus it didn't even matter!

Then the Lord taught me how to see what was in my "cup" and how to keep it full. Then He taught me how to pour it out on people. THEN things really got into HIGH gear! Whenever I would give everything away, I would get more. The faster I'd pour it out, the more He'd stretch me and give me more. All my gifts got more acute and stronger the more I used them and shared them. That's God's economy. That's how He does things. The widow that gives her last two cents, gets blessed the most. Whoever is most sacrificial, without thought of receiving in return, is the one with the pure heart that He blesses the most.

If you go pouring yourself out SO THAT you'll be blessed and get more power, your motives are all wrong and you'll probably get something really nasty to come live inside of you. You need to do it like Jesus – just because they have a need and you're willing, even if you don't get it back. If they need all my Peace, they can have it. If the Lord says to give them ALL my ability to hear the voice of God even if I might never get it back, they can have it. The more obedient you are, the more He'll ask you to sacrifice. The more you give sacrificially, the more He'll replace it with.

On August 24, 2006, I was doing something else and the Lord stopped me and reminded me of Joel 2:28:

"And afterward, I will pour out my Spirit on all flesh. Your sons and daughters will prophesy, your old men will dream dreams, your young men will see visions."

Really clearly He said, "You know, I've been doing that all along."

Well, yeah, people have been having dreams and visions since the beginning. So it's not like His Spirit hasn't been doing stuff. "Ok, so, Lord, what's the difference? Just the quantity poured out in the last days?"

"Yeah, lots more than you can imagine."

"OK, so Lord, when are the Spring and Latter rains going to fall at the same time? When does this start?"

"As soon as you start pouring My Spirit out on all flesh."

"HUH!?!? WE are the Early and Latter Rain? WE are the vehicle to pour Your Spirit out?!"

"Yep."

"How can that be, Lord?!"

"I told you and I showed you, endless rivers of living water will spring up from inside you. The more you give, the more you will get. The faster you pour it out, the faster it gets replaced. The more you sacrifice, the bigger your cup of Jesus."

"So if we just teach the Church how to pour out their spirit, we'll get this show on the road?"

"Yep. I've been waiting a long time for you guys to start sharing and stop hoarding what I give you. You're all lukewarm and stagnant because your cups aren't being poured out. You've settled on your lees."

WOW!! That just shocked me! I already understood about the cups and I'd seen the fruit of it over and over, but I never connected that WE were the ones that were supposed to take His Spirit to all flesh! That's all we're waiting for! As soon as the Church stops feeding their bodies and their brains and starts feeding their SPIRIT, we're full on into the big harvest. That's why people are dropping out of churches in droves. Not because they don't have enough to eat or enough to fill their brain – but because they are POOR IN SPIRIT and defenseless against the onslaught of the enemy. They have no power and don't know how to get any. So many of the denominations are powerless and neutered and filled with sick, dying people that can only depend on prescriptions and doctors. We're not looking to God for anything anymore. We don't need Him because we think we are rich, but really we are wretched, pitiful, poor, blind and naked – and lukewarm. Just like Revelation 3:14-22 said we would be.

That last statement is a reference to Zephaniah which is end times prophecy:

Zephaniah 1:12-13 – *And it shall come to pass at that time, that I will search Jerusalem with candles, and punish the men that are settled on their lees: that say in their heart, The LORD will not do good, neither will he do evil. 13 Therefore their goods shall become a booty, and their houses a desolation: they shall also build houses, but not inhabit them; and they shall plant vineyards, but not drink the wine thereof.*

They don't think God is even paying attention, but He's going to take everything away from them. When wine isn't poured out from one container to the other, nasty stuff happens to it. The process of pouring it out purifies and clarifies it. If it just sits (on it's lees), it's practically undrinkable. His reference about lukewarm and stagnant is to Rev 3:16 – *So, because you are lukewarm—neither hot nor cold—I am about to spit you out of my mouth.*

Lots of people don't understand this because they think we should all be HOT for Jesus. They don't get the historical context. Most folks didn't have running water like we do. Any hunter or agricultural person knows that hot water is from a hot spring, it's healing and healthful. Cold water is running water, it's clear and clean. Lukewarm water is stagnant and green on top. If you drink lukewarm water out in a forest, it will probably kill you. So Jesus is saying, "Be either healing or refreshing, but don't be stagnant or I'll spew you out. I don't care which, just be IN MOTION."

The wine that has settled on it's lees has been stagnant for too long and is useless. Whatever we have, we need to be pouring it out on those around us so that we stay "stirred up" and in motion.

The Lord showed me a picture of what the Church should be. Most folks will recognize it. We should be like the pyramid of champagne glasses at a wedding – so that when the Lord pours into the top one it just overflows and fills all the ones below it. Then everyone is constantly getting filled and refilled and staying in motion. Everyone shares with each as they have a need and from the riches of their spirit gives to all. It's exactly what the Book of Acts is all about. Sharing your money is a BY-PRODUCT of having shared your spirit. Share your money all you like, it's still not going to be like the Book of Acts because you'll be fed, but spiritually powerless.

Which is more loving? That you would lay down your physical life or your spiritual life for a friend? This earthly life is like a blade of grass or a flower that fades, but the eternal, the spiritual is where our focus should always be!

Are you getting it? Do you see it yet? People are leaving the churches because they are powerless and don't see anything there that will FILL the void inside of them. That's because we're not really feeding their spirit, we're feeding their brain and their soulish nature (and their body) and they know the difference. It's not working. Whose idea could it have been that we would stop feeding the spirit and focus entirely on the soul and the brain? That we would focus on legalism and Self instead of teaching them to just be full of Jesus? Hmmm. Tree of the Knowledge of Good and Evil sound familiar?

> 2 Timothy 3:1-7 – *1 But mark this: There will be terrible times in the last days. 2 People will be lovers of themselves, lovers of money, boastful, proud, abusive, disobedient to their parents, ungrateful, unholy, 3 without love, unforgiving, slanderous, without self-control, brutal, not lovers of the good, 4 treacherous, rash, conceited, lovers of pleasure rather than lovers of God— 5 having a form of godliness but denying its power. Have nothing to do with them. 6 They are the kind who worm their way into homes and gain control over weak-willed women, who are loaded down with sins and are swayed by all kinds of evil desires, 7 always learning but never able to acknowledge the truth.*

Ok, so if you look around America at the 41,000+ denominations we have now and at all the people that CALL themselves "Christians" – is it a stretch to say that we are pretty much all of those things? And worst of all we have a FORM of godliness, we say we're Christians, but we're denying the POWER thereof. That word is "dunamis" in the Greek, from which we get the word "dynamite" and we're going to talk about that later, but that's the fundamental problem we're having. People don't have any spiritual dynamite and they don't know how to get it. We are lovers of everything but God. We talk a good game, but when it comes down to it, we'd rather cancel church to see the Superbowl. We're always learning and never seeing the truth. Cramming our heads with all kinds of seminary knowledge and programs and curriculums, but not hearing the voice of God cut through all the clutter. We don't teach faith like a child, we teach faith like a smart-mouthed, self-willed teenager that thinks Dad is an idiot.

What does that passage say we're supposed to do with people like that? Have NOTHING to do with them. Between that passage and the one in Zephaniah, we probably ought to knock it off and say we're sorry. We need to start seeking God's face a LOT and let HIM direct all our paths for a change. And the first thing He'll probably tell you to do is find somebody to bless with the things that He's entrusted to you.

WHAT IS DUNAMIS?

Dunamis is the Greek word from which we get "dynamite". It is variously translated as power or might or strength or virtue, but is generally something bigger and stronger than normal man. It generally refers to something supernaturally strong and powerful. It is the dynamic thing that creates change in dramatic ways. It is used in four ways that I can find in the Word; to describe the normal, natural strength of a man; to describe the amazing, supernatural power of God in a man; to describe the supernatural power of the enemy; to describe the after-effects of the power having been moved from inside a man to outside a man (an act, miracles and wonders).

Dunamis (Strong's 1411) (some concordances say "dynamis")
1) strength power, ability
    a) inherent power, power residing in a thing by virtue of its nature, or which a person or thing exerts and puts forth
    b) power for performing miracles
    c) moral power and excellence of soul
    d) the power and influence which belong to riches and wealth
    e) power and resources arising from numbers
    f) power consisting in or resting upon armies, forces, hosts

Translated variously as: power 77, mighty work 11, strength 7, miracle 7, might 4, virtue 3, mighty 2, misc 9; 120 total occurences.

Sometimes it's a resident power bubbling under the surface and sometimes it's already been expressed in an act (miracle). I'm sure they were learning what to call all this stuff for the first time as the Lord left them to figure out what to do with a big cup full of dynamite!

Here is a foundational verse for you to consider as you go through this. Here we see something really important. Christ, the Messiah, IS the dunamis of God. Not only was He filled with it, He IS it. If we are filled with Jesus, we are filled with the dynamic power and wisdom of God! Get it? **If you are full of Jesus, you are full of dunamis.**

> I Corinthians 1:24 – *But unto them which are called, both Jews and Greeks, Christ the power (dunamis) of God, and the wisdom of God.*

I want to show that in the Christian, it's really the power of Christ in you to perform that for which He has called you. If the same power that was in Jesus is in us, then we need to get as much as we can of it and then we need to LET IT OUT!! Find something to point it at and blast away. The result will be more people filled with the power of God – and probably miracles like those that followed the early Church around.

> Mark 5:30 – *And Jesus, immediately knowing in himself that power* (dunamis) *had gone out of him, turned him about in the press, and said, Who touched my clothes?* (Also in Luke 8:46)

Here the woman with a blood disorder just touched the hem of Jesus' garment and He knew that power had drained out of Him. What kind of power? Dunamis – miracle working, supernatural power. She didn't just bump into Him, she sucked the power out of His cup! He hadn't willed it, she just took it.

31

Here it is again:

> Luke 6:19 – *And the whole multitude sought to touch him: for there went power* (dunamis) *out of him, and healed [them] all.*

There's something about making contact. It wasn't enough to just see Him from across the road. People wanted Jesus to touch them or they wanted to touch Him. He went around laying hands on the sick. He sent the disciples out with the Great Commission instructing them to lay hands on the sick. (Mark 16) The physical contact is important somehow, but not critical. They didn't have faith enough to get healed without it, but Jesus heals some people without touching them at all or even being in the same town. In Acts 5:15 Peter's shadow is healing people! In Acts 19:12 even handkerchiefs and aprons that had touched Paul were healing people and delivering them of evil spirits! The dunamis of the Spirit of God is transferable. It's a force that endures on people and objects.

Here we see Jesus impart specific flavors of it to His disciples: (deliverance and healing)

> Luke 9:1 – *Then he called his twelve disciples together, and gave them power* (dunamis) *and authority over all devils, and to cure diseases.*

But that was just a warm-up for the big stuff that came later:

> Acts 1:8 – *But ye shall receive power* (dunamis), *after that the Holy Ghost is come upon you: and ye shall be witnesses unto me both in Jerusalem, and in all Judaea, and in Samaria, and unto the uttermost part of the earth.*

OK, they had already received SOME dunamis in Luke 9:1, so this is more. So the Upper Room in Acts 2 is NOT the first time they get the power of the Holy Spirit in them. They could have gone and spread the Gospel when Jesus left, but He was very clear that they needed to wait until the Holy Spirit came. But they already had some Holy Spirit. Yeah, but they had to wait. Why? For the really BIG dose that would empower them in a great big way! Not just healing and deliverance, but the full spectrum of stuff that they were going to need. And when it happens they get far more than they could ever have imagined possible! They get great big cups full of Jesus all in one dose. They start speaking in other languages, singing and worshiping God all the time, they rejoice in afflictions, they share all their stuff, they prophecy, they evangelize, they reason with the religious authorities – in short, they are a WHOLE lot more like Jesus then they used to be. How can that be? Because they got a whole lot more Jesus IN them all of a sudden!

It was clear that this power is supernatural. Here Peter speaks sarcastically about it, with the obvious response to his rhetorical question that, of course, there is no way that their OWN human "dunamis" could do such a thing.

> Acts 3:12 – *And when Peter saw [it], he answered unto the people, Ye men of Israel, why marvel ye at this? or why look ye so earnestly on us, as though by our own power* (dunamis) *or holiness we had made this man to walk?*

Here are a bunch more examples. I don't have space here, look them all up in context, but the point is that the disciples were FULL of a supernatural miracle working power and it was the power of God. Sometimes the dunamis is put into action in the form of miracles. Rather than just an internal force, someone skilled with their weaponry systems has focused it and pushed it out at a particular target with amazing results! This is what spread the Gospel so fast!

> Acts 4:7 – *And when they had set them in the midst, they asked, By what power* (dunamis), *or by what name, have ye done this?*

Acts 4:33 – *And with great power* (dunamis) *gave the apostles witness of the resurrection of the Lord Jesus: and great grace was upon them all.*

Acts 6:8 – *And Stephen, full of faith and power* (dunamis), *did great wonders and miracles among the people.*

Acts 8:10 – *To whom they all gave heed, from the least to the greatest, saying, This man is the great power* (dunamis) *of God.*

Acts 10:38 – *How God anointed Jesus of Nazareth with the Holy Ghost and with power* (dunamis): *who went about doing good, and healing all that were oppressed of the devil; for God was with him.*

Acts 2:22 – *Ye men of Israel, hear these words; Jesus of Nazareth, a man approved of God among you by miracles* (dunamis) *and wonders and signs, which God did by him in the midst of you, as ye yourselves also know:*

Acts 19:11 – *And God wrought special miracles* (dunamis) *by the hands of Paul:*

Acts 8:13 – *Then Simon himself believed also: and when he was baptized, he continued with Philip, and wondered, beholding the miracles* (dunamis) *and signs which were done.*

I Corinthians 12:10 – *To another the working of miracles* (dunamis); *to another prophecy; to another discerning of spirits; to another [diverse] kinds of tongues; to another the interpretation of tongues:*

2 Corinthians 12:12 – *Truly the signs of an apostle were wrought among you in all patience, in signs, and wonders, and mighty deeds* (dunamis).

Galatians 3:5 – *He therefore that ministereth to you the Spirit, and worketh miracles* (dunamis) *among you, [doeth he it] by the works of the law, or by the hearing of faith?*

Romans 1:4 – *And declared [to be] the Son of God with power* (dunamis), *according to the spirit of holiness, by the resurrection from the dead:*

Philippians 3:10 – *That I may know him, and the power* (dunamis) *of his resurrection, and the fellowship of his sufferings, being made conformable unto his death;*

Romans 1:16 – *For I am not ashamed of the gospel of Christ: for it is the power* (dunamis) *of God unto salvation to every one that believeth ; to the Jew first, and also to the Greek.*

I Corinthians 1:18 – *For the preaching of the cross is to them that perish foolishness; but unto us which are saved it is the power* (dunamis) *of God.*

Did you see that? The GOSPEL is the dunamis of God. Not the "Purpose Driven Life" or "How to Win Friends and Influence People" or "Chicken Soup for the Christian Soul." The GOSPEL is the dunamis of God! Stop arguing about doctrine and secondary issues and self-help stuff and start preaching the Gospel and you'll see the power of God show up! It doesn't matter how long you can lecture about who wrote the book of Hebrews or archaeological discoveries that prove the Old Testament or the problems with the DaVinci Code. The power of God proves itself when it shows up. Just preach the Gospel, that's where the power of God lies. In the preaching of the CROSS is the dunamis of God!

Romans 15:13 – *Now the God of hope fill you with all joy and peace in believing, that ye may abound in hope, through the power* (dunamis) *of the Holy Ghost.*

Romans 15:19 – *Through mighty* (dunamis) *signs and wonders, by the power* (dunamis) *of the Spirit of God; so that from Jerusalem, and round about unto Illyricum, I have fully preached the gospel of Christ.*

The miraculous things that were done were not in their own power, but in the dynamic power of the Spirit of God when they FULLY preached the Gospel of Christ. Is that what we are seeing in America? I don't think so.

I Corinthians 2:4-5 – *And my speech and my preaching [was] not with enticing words of man's wisdom, but in demonstration of the Spirit and of power* (dunamis): *That your faith should not stand in the wisdom of men, but in the power* (dunamis) *of God.*

Boy, wouldn't THAT be a nice change from most of the sermons we've heard?! When are we going to get back to that?! As a percentage, how much of what's said in "church" is "enticing words of man's wisdom" and how much is "demonstration of the Spirit and of power"? If that stuff (dunamis) isn't for today, then all we've got left are "enticing words of man's wisdom" and I think I'd rather be an atheist. What's the point really?

I Corinthians 4:19-20 – *But I will come to you shortly, if the Lord will, and will know, not the speech of them which are puffed up, but the power* (dunamis) *For the kingdom of God [is] not in word, but in power* (dunamis)

I Corinthians 4:19 says that Paul is NOT going to test their doctrine or their head knowledge or the skillfulness of their speech making, he's going to test their dunamis. How much supernatural power is coming out of them? Do you do that? Do you test the dunamis of those who are speaking or the quality of their wisdom of man? Have you ever even SEEN dunamis in action? Come on, honestly, have you seen someone preach with such an anointing that people are wailing in fear and conviction because they could see the gates of hell open up under their feet? THAT is dunamis! That is what Peter got from 3,000 people when he preached his very first sermon (Acts 2) under the dunamis of God. And he didn't have any notes or commentaries or prepare ahead of time!

> 2 Corinthians 1:8 – *For we would not, brethren, have you ignorant of our trouble which came to us in Asia, that we were pressed out of measure, above strength* (dunamis)*, insomuch that we despaired even of life :*

If they despaired unto life, it wasn't just their own strength, even the power of God in them was waning thin. They're cups were drained of all the dunamis they had.

> 2 Corinthians 4:7 – *But we have this treasure in earthen vessels, that the excellency of the power* (dunamis) *may be of God, and not of us.*

> 2 Corinthians 12:9 – *And he said unto me, My grace is sufficient for thee: for my strength* (dunamis) *is made perfect in weakness. Most gladly therefore will I rather glory in my infirmities, that the power* (dunamis) *of Christ may rest upon me.*

When you have no strength of your own, then can the DUNAMIS of God be made perfect in your weakness. So glory and rejoice in infirmities SO THAT the DUNAMIS of CHRIST may rest upon you. The less YOU in your cup, the more JESUS can fit!

Want to hear it again?

> 2 Corinthians 13:4 – *For though he was crucified through weakness, yet he liveth by the power* (dunamis) *of God. For we also are weak in him, but we shall live with him by the power* (dunamis) *of God toward you.*

Lots more. Here are a few more examples of His power in us.

Ephesians 1:19 – *And what [is] the exceeding greatness of his power* (dunamis) *to us-ward who believe, according to the working of his mighty power* (kratos – dominion/authority, Strongs #2904) ,

Ephesians 3:16 – *That he would grant you, according to the riches of his glory, to be strengthened with might* (dunamis) *by his Spirit in the inner man;*

Ephesians 3:20 – *Now unto him that is able to do exceeding abundantly above all that we ask or think, according to the power* (dunamis) *that worketh in us,*

Colossians 1:11 – *Strengthened with all might* (dunamis), *according to his glorious power* (kratos – dominion/ authority, #2904), *unto all patience and long-suffering with joyfulness;*

2 Thessalonians 1:11 – *Wherefore also we pray always for you, that our God would count you worthy of [this] calling, and fulfill all the good pleasure of [his] goodness, and the work of faith with power* (dunamis):

2 Timothy 1:7 – *For God hath not given us the spirit of fear; but of power* (dunamis), *and of love, and of a sound mind.*

2 Timothy 1:8 – *Be not thou therefore ashamed of the testimony of our Lord, nor of me his prisoner: but be thou partaker of the afflictions of the gospel according to the power* (dunamis) *of God;*

2 Peter 1:3 – *According as his divine power* (dunamis) *hath given unto us all things that [pertain] unto life and godliness, through the knowledge of him that hath called us to glory and virtue:*

The enemy has supernatural power (dunamis) too.

> Luke 10:19 – *Behold , I give unto you power to tread on serpents and scorpions, and over all the power* (dunamis) *of the enemy: and nothing shall by any means hurt you.*

> Revelation 13:2 – *And the beast which I saw was like unto a leopard, and his feet were as [the feet] of a bear, and his mouth as the mouth of a lion: and the dragon gave him his power* (dunamis), *and his seat, and great authority.*

> Revelation 17:13 – *These have one mind, and shall give their power* (dunamis) *and strength unto the beast.*

> Revelation 18:3 – *For all nations have drunk of the wine of the wrath of her fornication, and the kings of the earth have committed fornication with her, and the merchants of the earth are waxed rich through the abundance* (dunamis) *of her delicacies.*

There is YOUR dunamis and then there is GOD'S dunamis! Which do you want to be FULL of? In these three verses we see dunamis used in terms of physical strength, ability or capacity or quantity – but not supernatural power.

> Matthew 25:15 – *And unto one he gave five talents, to another two, and to another one; to every man according to his several ability* (dunamis); *and straightway took his journey.*

> 2 Corinthians 1:8 – *For we would not, brethren, have you ignorant of our trouble which came to us in Asia, that we were pressed out of measure, above strength* (dunamis), *insomuch that we despaired even of life :*

> 2 Corinthians 12:9 – *And he said unto me, My grace is sufficient for thee: for my strength* (dunamis) *is made perfect in weakness. Most gladly therefore will I rather glory in my infirmities, that the power* (dunamis) *of Christ may rest upon me.*

Here we see the contrast between OUR strength and the dunamis of God!

> Revelation 12:10 – *And I heard a loud voice saying in heaven, Now is come salvation, and strength* (dunamis), *and the kingdom of our God, and the power of his Christ: for the accuser of our brethren is cast down, which accused them before our God day and night* .

> Revelation 15:8 – *And the temple was filled with smoke from the glory of God, and from his power* (dunamis); *and no man was able to enter into the temple, till the seven plagues of the seven angels were fulfilled.*

> Revelation 19:1 – *And after these things I heard a great voice of much people in heaven, saying, Alleluia; Salvation, and glory, and honour, and power* (dunamis), *unto the Lord our God:*

Which one do you think you'd rather be filled with?! The Word says that WE each are the temple not built by human hands. (Mark 14:58) That means that God's Spirit dwells within us. Well I want my temple, my body, my spirit, so full of the cloud of the glory of God and His power that nothing else would be able to enter this temple! Is that possible? He says it is and I believe it. My personal experience is that it truly does work just like that. You can get your "cup" so crammed full of Jesus that nothing else can fit. Keep reading and you'll learn how.

It's the dunamis of God that keeps us through faith unto salvation.

> I Peter 1:3-5 – *Blessed [be] the God and Father of our Lord Jesus Christ, which according to his abundant mercy hath begotten us again unto a lively hope by the resurrection of Jesus Christ from the dead, To an inheritance incorruptible, and undefiled, and that fadeth*

not away, reserved in heaven for you, who are kept by the power (dunamis) *of God through faith unto salvation ready to be revealed in the last time.*

It is Christ in us, the power of God in us, that keeps us through faith inside the power of salvation. It is dunamis that helps us navigate the narrow path. Without it, we are without hope.

Now we get to some hard ones. How about this one that nobody likes to talk about?

Hebrews 6:4-6 – *For [it is] impossible for those who were once enlightened, and have tasted of the heavenly gift, and were made partakers of the Holy Ghost, And have tasted the good word of God, and the powers* (dunamis) *of the world to come, If they shall fall away, to renew them again unto repentance; seeing they crucify to themselves the Son of God afresh, and put [him] to an open shame.*

OK, so who is it that they're talking about in this verse? Those who have been enlightened **AND** tasted the heavenly gift **AND** were partakers in the Holy Ghost **AND** have tasted the good word of God **AND** held the spiritual, supernatural power of the world to come. If THOSE people should fall away, it's impossible to renew and restore them. This isn't about people that got saved at youth camp in 8th grade and then sinned again. This is a VERY high standard. These are people who have experienced the FULLNESS of God and still turned away.

To tell you the truth, I don't think we've seen any of these people yet. I think this is a prophetic pronouncement about someone yet to come. I don't think I've ever met or heard of anyone that met all those qualifications. We have people that have sampled, have nibbled at the power of the world to come, but nobody has really walked in it and been fully enlightened and truly tasted the "good" word of God in clarity and truth and fullness. I think this is about those who are coming, the man-child remnant of Revelation that is the first-fruits of the harvest to come. (But I could be wrong.)

OK, that's a lot of stuff about dunamis! Are you getting it yet? It's the power of God in you and the more you have, the more you can do stuff with it. If you have a little you get faith and salvation and joy and peace and hope. If you have a lot, you get the bigger Gifts like healing and miracles and prophecy. Plus, the more you have, the more you're like Jesus and the more persecution and affliction is going to come – and the more you're going to glory in it. I know that's just nutty, but that's the way Kingdom Economics works. Want a bigger cup of Jesus? Give more away, suffer more, fast more, die to self more. Want a big cup of Jesus so you can impress your friends with how you can heal people or so you can make money? Fat chance. He'll probably turn you over to something really ugly. People might get healed, but it's going to cost you. Those are the folks that hear, "Get away from me I never knew you." when the sheep and the goat judgement comes (Matt. 25). Yeah, you did stuff with the Gifts He gave you, but you made it about YOU instead of about HIM.

Here's something to think about. (I know we just did this earlier, but please humor me. It's important.)

> 2Tim 3:1-5 – *For men shall be lovers of their own selves, covetous, boasters, proud, blasphemers, disobedient to parents, unthankful, unholy, without natural affection, trucebreakers, false accusers, incontinent, fierce, despisers of those that are good, traitors, heady, highminded, lovers of pleasures more than lovers of God; Having a form of godliness, but denying the power* (dunamis) *thereof: from such turn away.*

Are you following leaders in the "church" that are like this? Are YOU like this?

What is a "form" of godliness anyway? Well, that would be like going to church, wearing a cross, having a fishy on your car, saying you love Jesus and then doing whatever you want, even if it hurts Him. So what is "denying the power thereof"? Well, that's like denying that the Gifts of the Spirit are for today and are real and that we need them. That's like saying God isn't really talking to us or doing stuff anymore, so the Christian life consists of putting on our Sunday show and then going home and watching the football game. That's like trusting doctors and drugs and insurance more than you trust God. That's like storing up treasure on earth instead of treasure in heaven. That's like having no fear of the Lord and not believing He is really going to talk to you when you pray. That's like being more afraid of a Ouija Board than trembling at the thought that you might be taking Communion unworthily. That kind of stuff.

What does "from such turn away" mean? Well that means REPENT and RUN from them. And if you are one of them, TURN and run from yourself and the old man that was in love with the world more than in love with God. If your religion is dead, it's probably because there is no DUNAMIS of God left in it. If you are exhibiting those traits in that verse then God is probably not in you. At least not in any sufficient enough measure to outweigh the YOU in you. You are going your own way and are a lover of Self. Repent and turn and beg for the power of God that will keep you through faith unto salvation.

If our "churches" are filled with these kinds of leaders how do we know who to follow? How can we tell who are the real ones?

Ephesians 3:7 – *Whereof I was made a minister* (diakonos), *according to the gift of the grace* (charis) *of God given unto me by the effectual working* (energeia) *of his power* (dunamis).

That is: "I was made a DIAKONOS (deacon, elder) according to the CHARIS (gift of grace) given unto me by the ENERGEIA (effectual, supernatural working and energy) of His DUNAMIS (power)."

For real?! Let's get this straight. Didn't Paul get to be an elder because he went to seminary and got voted on by a search committee? Didn't Paul get to be an elder because he was a good businessman and wise in the ways of the world? Because he contributed to the building fund? Because of the eloquence of his preaching style? Because he was the co-author of a new book that would forever outsell every other book on the planet?

NO! You get to be a TRUE deacon/minister/elder because you are MADE ONE by the Gift of Grace that is supernaturally given to you by the Power of God! In short, whoever has the biggest cup of Jesus is probably the "Elder." In some congregations I've visited, that's the little old lady in the back in the wheelchair. They would never think to let her preach, but when she prays, everything in heaven stops so God can hear her REALLY clearly. SHE is the one that needs to be dispensing the grace of God to everybody. She's the one that knows how to get full of Jesus and stay full. Sometimes a little kid has the biggest, purest cup of Jesus. I've seen it all. God uses the most unlikely people. Occasionally it's even the pastor!

All the people that SAY they are elders but GOD didn't put them in place by His ENERGEIA and confirm it with His DUNAMIS are not really elders at all. If this really is God's criteria for who we should be listening to and who should be leading, we're in big trouble. Look around, we have a huge shortage of DUNAMIS in the Church of America.

2 Corinthians 12:12 – *Truly the signs of an apostle were wrought among you in all patience, in signs, and wonders, and mighty deeds* (dunamis).

A true God-anointed apostle is not someone who has a big ministry or just claims to be an apostle. An apostle is not an apostle because he has lots of dreams and visions and a gift for administration. You will know they are an apostle because of their supernatural patience, the signs and wonders and the mighty deeds that follow them. You will know they are an apostle because they have a great big cup of Jesus and just LOVE to sacrificially pour it out on all the people around them. You will know they are an apostle because they don't make it about THEM, they point everyone to Jesus. They need to know God up close and personal and be someone who is directed by God, not by any man. They know how to depend on the Father fully and believe in faith that He is sufficient for any need.

You will probably also know they are an apostle because of the really surprising level of persecution they seem to endure everywhere they go. If they are the biggest cups, then the enemy wants to stop them the most.

Do we still have apostles today? Yes. There is no indication that we don't. An "apostle" is one who is sent out. Any missionary or church-planter would qualify, but you'll know they're from God by the dunamis that follows them.

There were the original 13 Apostles (capital "A"), but there are more than 20 people in the Bible that are referred to as apostles – including women. It was set as one of the multiple callings of ministry for the establishment and proper functioning of the church and there is no indication we stopped needing them. We'll talk more about that in another chapter.

To tie all of this up, get more dunamis. Get as much as you can and be a good steward of it.

Don't know how to get more? Keep reading.

**EXCERPTED FROM 'JAMES DUNN,
SIGN GIFT MINISTRY' BY W.V. GRANT SR**

JAMES DUNN
HEALING REVIVALIST OF THE EARLY 20TH CENTURY.

"I pastored the Pentecostal Holiness church there for two years before this ministry came to me. I had been fasting, and praying, and I had been reminding God. I believe God wants us to remind Him about the promises He has made to us, to call his attention to them. So I was reminding God that when I was employed in a responsible position for the government, we gave our men the best tools on earth possible to work with, so that they could do their job right. I told God that if we as mere human beings could give good tools to our laborers, how much better tools could He give us to work for the Kingdom of Christ. I continued praying in that way, and begging God for the gifts. Just imagine! I would cry: the tears rolling down my face. I would fast until the preachers in Princeton remarked that my clothes hung on me like a sack, because I had lost so much weight. They thought that the clothes had belonged to someone else. I don't know how many pounds I did lose. I was way down in weight."

"One day I was just in a big way of praying; tears streaming down my face as I was alone before God. I was asking Him again to give me the gifts of the Spirit. A voice spoke to me and said, 'Just a minute.' And I stopped, and a voice spoke again, and said, 'DON'T BEG FOR THE GIFTS OF THE SPIRIT, PRAY TO BE MORE LIKE ME.' I said, Why Jesus, I had never thought of it in that manner, what do you mean, pray to be more like you? And the voice said to me, **'THE GIFTS OF THE SPIRIT WILL OPERATE IN YOUR LIFE, IF YOU ARE FULL OF JESUS.'** So I began to pray that I would be just exactly like Jesus."

"Then one night while I was lying in bed and my wife was asleep, something happened. I was meditating on the glories and graciousness of God, and upon the things I needed from Him, and all at once, the Great Presence of God began to flood into the room. He came in such a supernatural way that the room was filled with His Glory. A great feeling of ecstasy and glory swept over me, and saturated my very body, mind, and soul. I began to get afraid, because when you get that close to God, something happens to you. I began to draw back from this Wonderful Force, and when I did it left. **Then I realized I had made a mistake in drawing back.** The next few days, I began to pray as I had never prayed. In about 3 or 4 nights I was lying in the bed again and I was meditating and praising the Lord, and asking Him for help and power in my life. All at once, this great feeling began to come into the room again."

"The very room and atmosphere lighted up. There didn't seem to be any room for me there any longer, because God so completely filled the place. As I lay there, I lost all movement of my body other than my eyes. The Great Force of God moved down across my bed, and overshadowed me, and I felt the strangest, and most wonderful feeling. **From my very fingertips, it began to move into my hands, and up my arms. I felt as if I were holding 220 volts in each hand, and it began to surge back and forth through my body. Then**

and there in that room, while this was taking place the old me was leaving, and the new me was coming in."

"From that night on my life was different. Many remarked how completely my ministry had changed. I had a positive message - a message, that had fire in it. God talked to me, and told me that if I would preach the message of deliverance, He would heal the sick. He would give me the Power to cast out devils. As I listened to this COMMISSION from the Lord, **His power surged through me, and my arm happened to touch my wife's body, and it almost caused her to jump completely out of the bed.** That night God began doing things. He revealed to me the people's conditions and diseases through the mighty Spirit of discernment. I found I was a different individual. God showed me things that I thought were impossible for a person to see or understand. He would show me the individual that was suffering, what they had, and He would direct me to them. After I had prayed for them, they would be healed of every disease."

('James Dunn, Sign Gift Ministry' by W.V. Grant Sr)

WHAT DO WE DO FIRST?
BE A M*A*S*H

Before we start trying to pass out spiritual gifts, we better be sure that we're all cleaned out – personally and collectively. You have to purify the Temple first. The most common thing that I've seen in all my visiting different denominations is that almost universally there is a tendency toward putting on programs and ignoring the individual. The bigger the congregation, the greater the tendency. In reality how that manifests always includes a statement about family and concern for the individual but then it's offset and negated by the reality of a structure seemingly engineered to disregard individual needs. However unconscious this may be, the reality is clearly that millions of Christians are NOT walking in the fullness of Christ or worse, walking around with massive oppressions that continue to go untreated. We really shouldn't even try to go "dialing up" people that have lots of open doorways.

There are TONS of people leaving the institutional churches. Millions of them per year. Why? Because they don't feel like their individual needs are getting addressed. They may sit through a good sermon that has some life application, but they don't see or feel the radical transformation that should come as a part of the normal Christian life. Or worse, they have a crisis or a need and nobody in the "church" responds appropriately.

We are NOT honoring God. We are singing and dancing and pretending everything is fine while people are bleeding to death in the pews (not to mention in the streets). Listen to me, God does NOT want you to praise and worship Him while you're ignoring the person sitting next to you who is having a crisis! It DOES NOT bring Him honor for you to raise your hands and tell Him how great He is while you FAIL to act like Him and heal those nearest to you. Heal them – or at least TREAT them – and THEN you can go praising and worshiping and telling Him how great He is. He just DOES NOT want to hear you singing while you're ignoring people that are crying inside! Your prayers are going to bounce off of the brass over your head until you act like Jesus. Just knock it off – or else. He's not going to ignore their cries much longer.

The church should be like the TV show "M*A*S*H". If they're having a party and someone shouts "Choppers!" then the music stops and everybody rushes into action to do triage. That means rapidly identifying and categorizing the wounded based on needs - the bleeding, sucking chest wounds go first, then the broken legs, then the scratches. AFTER everybody is treated and in Recovery – THEN you can go back to your party. But what kind of hospital would you be if you let them bleed to death in the compound because you refuse to stop singing and dancing because you had a schedule to keep?!

You planned for this party to take an hour and a half and, by golly, you're going to stay on time no matter what.

Even when Jesus was right in the middle of a great sermon and had them all in the palm of His hand, if a paralyzed guy dropped down out of the roof, Jesus STOPPED TALKING and healed him. THEN He could go on with his sermon - AND everybody was REALLY impressed because of the miracle that had just happened in front of them! I'm not sure which would be the bigger miracle in some churches, that a paralytic rose and walked away or that the pastor stopped in the middle of a sermon!

The people of God need to be trained up in how to rapidly identify the physical, emotional and spiritual warfare oppressing and killing their brethren and they need to be empowered to go and treat them on the spot. The music needs to stop until EVERYBODY in your camp is bandaged up. "Church" will not be **The Church** until it stops being a show and starts being a hospital, first and foremost. The reason it's not that now is because we abdicated to paid leadership to do all the work for us and they can't possibly keep up. In fairness (to us), many of them got to liking it and now don't trust the Body to help them - so it's a vicious cycle. But it's got to stop. The Body has to learn to care for the Body, whether or not there is a paid staffer. We need the Gifts of Discernment of Spirits and Knowledge operating in force and we need to get back to fulfilling the Great Commission - first by cleaning up the messes in our own congregations, then by GOING. We can't wait for them to COME - cause when we do, they're mostly not staying, and it's because they're not getting healed (which is because we're not acting like Jesus).

If any of this stuff has convicted you and you realize you played a part in sustaining a system that hasn't been working or you ever ignored someone that was bleeding because you had your own agenda, now would be a good time to find a quiet place, hit your knees and say you're sorry. Crying helps God know you're serious. You might also want to admit it publicly to the people affected. How are they ever going to learn how to repent really good if somebody doesn't show them? Don't wait for somebody else to do it. It has to start with you.

If you kneel down and repent and cry in front of them, it might just start a revival. Some of them have never seen ANYBODY do that before! (If nothing else, it will give them something new to gossip about.) :-)

NEED A SPIRITUAL TUNE-UP?

First, this is aimed at people that already have Jesus, but the process is the same regardless. A person who is lost could turn their life over and push through lots of the steps right away and be that much more effective sooner. It's just a matter of hunger level and God's sense of your preparedness. The goal is immediate radical transformation, not gradual incremental change culminating in perfection after death. We believe that it's possible that God can heal and deliver and restore and sanctify instantly and we're going to aim for <u>that</u>. If He chooses to take longer, that's fine, but we're going to ASK for maximum change in minimum time - even if it hurts. Which it will.

Typically, we would take a hard look at each of the three factors; Body, Soul and Spirit. Asking the Holy Spirit to help us discern any areas where there is resistance to the will of Christ, we would "scan" through each layer looking for whatever the Lord would choose to reveal. It might be a physical illness that has a spiritual cause, it might be a soulish anger or bitterness or unforgiveness that is blocking Him and bringing down physical curses, or it might be a spiritual problem of diminished capacity for Him because of limitations or "filters" that have been placed on God. It might be a demonic oppression that has really old roots in abuse or addiction or some unresolved, past sin that opened a doorway and allowed legal ground for the enemy. All of these are resolvable within the scope of the power granted to us through Christ. Some can be settled nearly instantly and done away with once and for all. Many people have experienced through this process an immediately lightness at the removal of some old yokes of oppression. Some experience immediate physical changes as healing to their illnesses or removal of addictions comes at the same time. We want to allow God room to act in ANY way He sees fit. We don't want to put Him in a box anymore! We want to believe that He is big enough to conquer anything and that He wants us free. He is big enough, right? And He does want us fully free, right? All the way free? Of everything?

When you do a tune-up on a vehicle, you want to find anything that is keeping it from running at peak efficiency. A misalignment, a missing part, low fluids, bad filters, even burnt out bulbs - anything that needs to be changed or adjusted so that it can be renewed back to the way it was designed. It's all in Romans 12. In thanks for His mercy we offer our bodies as living sacrifices - holy, pleasing and acceptable - that is our spiritual act of worship.

So first, we have to be willing to offer our Body - the vehicle, and all that it holds - as a sacrifice. We need to be willing and we need to commit to hold NOTHING back anything. That verse does NOT say we offer half of our body as a living sacrifice – or even 90%. The whole thing needs to go on the altar. ALL means ALL.

Before we can do anything else, we need it to be a holy, pleasing and acceptable sacrifice. And since our sinfulness screams against our holiness, and our own nature confirms it, it's clear that only by the atoning Blood of Jesus is there any chance that we can be a pleasing and acceptable sacrifice. So before any tune-up is going to do any good, we need to scrub the whole thing down with the Blood of Jesus. You have to have acknowledged your needfulness for the Blood and asked Him to wash you clean of every sin.

Said less religiously, you have to tell Jesus you're sorry for all the bad stuff you let in and you have to really mean it - and you have to believe that His sacrifice on the cross was sufficient to wipe you clean. This IS NOT an acknowledgment that Jesus existed or that He was the Son of God - even the demons believe that. This is not a statement you repeat after someone else so that you can join a church. This is a full-on commitment to humble yourself before Him and to give yourself over to Him so that He can be in charge from now on. That you would like to bow down and let Him be who He is - Master, King, Commander, Ruler, Lord - in your life from now on. Fear of the Lord is the beginning of wisdom. Way too many churches are making it way too easy - and the result is sick, powerless, shackled, unwise people in the pews.

Ok, NOW you're an acceptable sacrifice. So what's next? Get up on the altar and shut up. You don't need to figure out your personal purpose. You don't need 40 days to figure out what YOU can do for God. You're the sacrifice! Get cleaned off, climb up on the altar and lay there naked. By doing this, by really doing this, really laying there naked – fully exposed and willing to accept anything that comes – you are most definitely NOT conforming to the "world".

When He's good and ready, He'll move on to the next step. Which is that He will take a big sword and begin to hack chunks of your head off and put His head on. It's painful at times and folks around you may not understand what's happening during that strange in-between time while you're trying to figure it all out and get the pieces of your head and His head to get on the same frequency. But eventually, unless you panic and jump off the altar, He will hack off all the bits that stand in His way and then you'll have the mind of Christ. He will have transformed you by the renewing of your mind. RE-newed, that is, back the way it was supposed to be when it was new. Back the way He designed it. Back in His image. Rebooted and set back to the defaults the way it was before you mangled it up and the "world's" viruses corrupted it. Read Matthew 18:1-4, Mark 10:15. He wants faith like a child.

Then and ONLY then will you know what is the pleasing, perfect will of God. And then you can go do it. It's not just so you can bask in the knowledge of what He wants, it's so you can OBEY. GO - reach, heal, save, deliver, free the captives. Do the stuff that's on HIS heart - and now that your mind is renewed and you know what is His will, it should be a lot easier. You probably won't need a committee or demographic studies or anything. If you didn't hold anything back, by this point, you're probably hearing Him really well and you don't really need any Man (or group of them) to tell you what God wants for you. And I can tell you this, it's going to cost you everything. But you won't miss any of it. Besides, none of it was yours anyway. But you better count the cost, because this is a hard walk. Job, family, money, comforts, control - all could be taken away or destroyed. If you pray to be like Jesus and He answers it, you'll be hated and ridiculed by the world. Guaranteed.

Sound like something you want to try? If you're lukewarm, it might just be better for you to stay where you are than to taste the goodness of God and then turn your back on it. Persecution is going to come with every step that gets you closer to walking in the fullness of Christ. But if you don't care what it costs and you're still willing, we can proceed.

Jesus affirmed repeatedly that these two commandments are the greatest. That if you understand and implement these, you have pretty well grasped the Kingdom of God.

Here it is quoted in three different Gospels: (Please go read them in context)

> Matthew 22:37-40 – *Jesus said unto him, Thou shalt love the Lord thy God with all thy heart, and with all thy soul, and with all thy mind. This is the first and great commandment. And the second [is] like unto it, Thou shalt love thy neighbour as thyself. On these two commandments hang all the law and the prophets.*

> Mark 12:30-31 – *And thou shalt love the Lord thy God with all thy heart, and with all thy soul, and with all thy mind, and with all thy strength: this [is] the first commandment. And the second [is] like, [namely] this, Thou shalt love thy neighbour as thyself. There is none other commandment greater than these.*

> Luke 10:27-28 – *And he answering said, Thou shalt love the Lord thy God with all thy heart, and with all thy soul, and with all thy strength, and with all thy mind; and thy neighbour as thyself. And he (Jesus) said unto him, Thou hast answered right: this do, and thou shalt live.*

So, it boils down to this - the most important command-ment, the most central task before us as individuals and as the Church, is to love God with every component of our being - Mind, Soul and Heart and to do it with all of our Strength. How are you doing with that? That's what we're going to find out. If you haven't got that one down, the second commandment - loving your neighbor as yourself - is going to be a pale imitation of what it should be. You will love them to the degree you love God. If you're clearly not loving your neighbor as you should, it's a pretty good indication that you're not loving the Lord your God with all your mind and soul and heart and strength. If you're loving your neighbor with 10% of your strength, then you're probably loving God with 10%. It's like a math equation, just plug in the percentage.

Submission to God x quantityN =
Manifestation of Love for Neighbor x quantityN

If they will know us by our love and we're not evidencing much love for each other (especially inside the Church) and for those in need, then we must not be very submitted to God. What other conclusion can you come to? Fear of the Lord is the beginning of wisdom. I know it stings a little, but try to embrace it. (Try Psalms 141:5-6)

Paul says this in 1 Thessalonians 5:23:

> *"And the very God of peace sanctify you wholly; and [I pray God] your whole spirit and soul and body be preserved blameless unto the coming of our Lord Jesus Christ."*

We are made of these three. Body, Soul and Spirit. and they are to all be in submission to Christ. All means ALL! Let's try one of those verses again:

Mark 12:30-31 – *And thou shalt love the Lord thy God with ALL thy heart, and with ALL thy soul, and with ALL thy mind, and with ALL thy strength: this [is] the first commandment. And the second [is] like, [namely] this, Thou shalt love thy neighbour as thyself. There is none other commandment greater than these.*

Before we go any further, now would be a good time for the WARNING label.

WARNING!

DANGER! DANGER!

Proceed at your own risk!

We will NOT be responsible for ANYTHING that happens from here forward. You have been warned.

We want you to be ABSOLUTELY clear that this is

<u>FOR</u> <u>SURE</u>, <u>NO</u> <u>DOUBT</u> <u>ABOUT</u> <u>IT</u> going to hurt <u>A</u> <u>LOT</u>.

You can drive 20 miles an hour and you probably won't get hurt too badly in an accident.

If you drive 200 miles an hour and you make a mistake, it's going to get really ugly.

This IS <u>NOT</u> for sissies!

If you have ANY desire in you to slow down, DO IT NOW! DO NOT GO THIS WAY!! DO NOT take our advice on this stuff!! It will totally transform your life and things you love will be ripped from you. Nothing – <u>NOTHING</u> – that you have will be your own any more.

So He can rebuild you His way, God will IMMEDIATELY start yanking chunks out of you. Probably stuff you really liked. The fire will get VERY hot!

If you even so much as TRY to do this in your own power, you're gonna be toast! <u>ONLY Jesus in you can get you through this.</u>

Last chance. Get out now! ALL the darkness WILL come for you!

We've seen it over and over. We <u>ARE</u> <u>NOT</u> kidding around!

If you miss a step you could end up on crack or beating your wife or drinking like a fish or in jail. We've seen it happen to good, Jesus-loving people who weren't <u>all</u> <u>the</u> <u>way</u> sold out. God will get you through, but it will hurt even more if you bail out. You BETTER mean it! We're serious.

We love you very much. We want to see you refined and purified and REALLY dangerous to the enemy, but we want you to be <u>FULLY READY</u> before you pull into the <u>Fast</u> <u>Lane!</u>

STILL HERE?

GREAT!

NOW GO BACK AND REREAD
THE WARNING AGAIN!

WE'RE TO WORK OUT OUR
SALVATION WITH FEAR AND
TREMBLING. HE'S SERIOUS.

OK? BACK AGAIN?

GOOD.

LET'S PROCEED.

SO WHICH PART OF <u>ALL</u> DON'T YOU UNDERSTAND?!

Where do you think you have an option to love Him "some"? Remember this old song? Have you really looked at it? How many times have you sung it and not really meant it? I know I did for years!

I Surrender All
by Judson W. Van DeVenter, 1896:

ALL to Jesus, I surrender; **ALL** to Him I freely give; I will **EVER** love and trust Him, In His presence **DAILY** live.

I surrender **ALL**, I surrender **ALL**, **ALL** to Thee, my blessed Savior, I surrender **ALL**.

ALL to Jesus I surrender; Humbly at His feet I bow, Worldly pleasures **ALL** forsaken; Take me, Jesus, take me now.

I surrender **ALL**, I surrender **ALL**, **ALL** to Thee, my blessed Savior, I surrender **ALL**.

ALL to Jesus, I surrender; Make me, Savior, **WHOLLY** Thine; Let me feel the Holy Spirit, Truly know that Thou art mine.

I surrender **ALL**, I surrender **ALL**, **ALL** to Thee, my blessed Savior, I surrender **ALL**.

ALL to Jesus, I surrender; Lord, I give myself to Thee; **FILL** me with Thy love and power; Let Thy blessing fall on me.

I surrender **ALL**, I surrender **ALL**, **ALL** to Thee, my blessed Savior, I surrender **ALL**.

ALL to Jesus I surrender; **NOW** I feel the sacred flame. O the joy of **FULL** salvation! Glory, glory, to His Name!

I surrender **ALL**, I surrender **ALL**, **ALL** to Thee, my blessed Savior, I surrender **ALL**.

A whole lot of us have been singing that but really meaning, "I surrender SOME." Or maybe, "I surrender more than that guy over there." There are certainly lots of leaders in the churches that aren't meaning it! Very few people really mean ALL. And yet that is the specific and direct command of God and affirmed three times by Jesus Himself as the most critical commandment of all. More than any doctrinal statement or theological construct or interpretation, we must do THAT. First and foremost in the Christian walk MUST BE a love for God that holds back nothing. Anything less means that you have missed the mark. Can there be <u>any</u> other interpretation? Where does the Bible say, "Invite Jesus into your heart and then do whatever you want."? Where does it say that you can give Him SOME and He won't mind. It says that God is a jealous God (Ex. 25:5, Ex. 34:14, Deut. 4:24; Deut. 5:9; Deut. 6:15; Josh. 24:19; Nahum 1:2; and elsewhere!). In fact, it says the Holy Spirit in us envies intensely when we give ourselves over to the world (James 4:4-5).

This is hard stuff, and not what you may be used to hearing, but I don't see how you can find any other interpretation. We're to work out our salvation with fear and trembling. How much fear and trembling do you have if you go down the aisle at youth camp in 8th grade and accept Jesus into your heart and you're all done? The "Narrow Path" has just GOT to be more narrow than that! In fact, I believe the VAST majority of church goers are not going to heaven at all. I believe we've been lied to for years about what it is that God really expects of us. The New Testament would be VERY short indeed if the path to heaven was as simple as, "Repeat this prayer after me ..." What's the point of all the rest of it if that's all it takes?

If you're still with me, the rest of this is going to be about helping you identify ANY areas of Body, Soul or Spirit that may yet be unsubmitted to God and doing whatever is necessary to bring them into full obedience with Christ. Bite down on something, this might hurt a little.

The enemy is going to try everything possible to keep you from walking this out. The darkness DOES NOT want to lose a single inch of ground! So let's pray this first:

> *Lord, don't let the enemy keep me from this. Don't let the enemy distract me or confuse me. Give me wisdom, Godly wisdom and as much of it as You think I can handle. Speak to me clearly and I'll follow. Please bind up anything in me or around me that would try to mess with me during this time. In the Name of Jesus. Amen.*

I like pictures, so let's start with this:

Holiness means EVERY piece of you is in obedience with Christ. Not just that you've made a "profession" of faith, but that you submit ALL of you to be bent to His will. With no reservation or evasion – nothing is off-limits to His control.

If there are parts of you that are not submitted, then you ARE NOT "filled" with the Holy Spirit. Stop telling people you're "Spirit-filled" if you're only half-full! Unless EVERY piece of you has been Baptized in the Holy Spirit, you're not all the way full. They have to have been crucified so that they can raise with Him in glory.

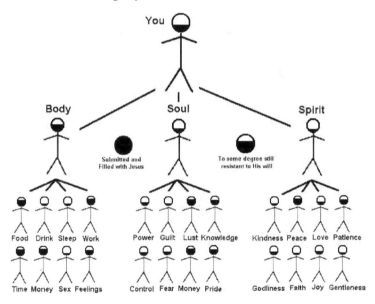

This is a very simple graphic, not at all meant to be thorough or all-inclusive. Let the Holy Spirit show you all the areas in your life that need addressing. I'm sure He wants to! For now, we're just going to hit a few so you can see how this works. If you're not hearing very well from God on what might be unsubmitted, just ask someone close to you – I'm sure they'll tell you the parts that don't look like Jesus. Spouses are good for that!

If we had lots of people in the churches with the gift of discernment of spirits, you could go to one of them and ask them what's messing with you and they could just tell you and help get it off. If you know somebody like that, by all means, get them in on this. But don't take ANYBODY'S word for anything. Check everything with God. Even if you can't normally hear God very well, I'm just SURE He wants to talk to you about THIS stuff! So you should be expecting that, as it relates to areas of your life that are unsubmitted, you're going to hear Him really well.

I suspect He's been waiting so long for you to ask Him what the problem is that as soon as you ask you're going to get LOTS of feedback. It may not be an audible thing, but somebody or some situation or a cloud or a little kid or a song on the radio or SOMETHING is going to be used to get through to you and show you the problem. Just EXPECT an answer and listen for it

Body

We are all jars of clay, vessels to hold His glory, cups of one sort or another. We are humble earthen vessels that are flawed and cracked in many ways and yet He pours His glory into us. We become the temple of His Spirit and He lives in us! Isn't that cool!!

Anyway, it's important first to understand that the Word commands us repeatedly to "be filled with the Spirit" and in the tense it uses it means "to be being filled" - a constant in-filling, a constant effort to keep our cups topped off. (The graphics here are from the full article "Fill My Cup, Lord." on the website – FellowshipOfTheMartyrs.com)

There are basically these options: (with lots of shades in between)

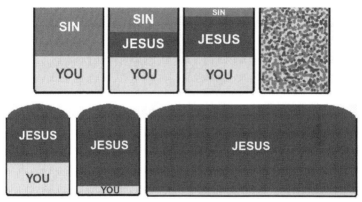

- You have NO JESUS.

- You have some JESUS and lots of SIN.

- You have more JESUS and a little SIN.

- You're all shook up by the World and "life" and can't figure out what's what.

- You're washed clean, but there's too much YOU.

- JESUS has killed off lots of YOU so He can increase and YOU can decrease.

- You've been a good steward, so He gave you a bigger cup and lots more JESUS.

And it's not a one-time thing. He's our Daily Bread, so you can move from one to the other fairly fluidly, even in the midst of one day. It's not a one-time thing just cause you went down the aisle and got "filled with the Spirit" one day. If you're not constantly STAYING FULL then you're going to drain off - or get lukewarm and stale. Over and over we're commanded to be full and to stay full – or to "be being filled". * And there's no point at which you shouldn't be striving for a bigger cup. We need Him in increasing measure every day to keep from being ineffective and unproductive (II Peter 1:8). You get a bigger cup by pouring yourself out on those in need, then getting refilled again.

* (Acts 2:4 *And they were all **filled** with the Holy Ghost, and began to speak with other tongues, as the Spirit gave them utterance.* Ephesians 3:19 *And to know the love of Christ, which passeth knowledge, that ye might be **filled** with all the **fullness** of God.* Colossians 1:9 *For this cause we also, since the day we heard [it], do not cease to pray for you, and to desire that ye might be **filled** with the knowledge of his will in all wisdom and spiritual understanding;* Ephesians 5:8 *And be not drunk with wine, wherein is excess; but be **filled** with the Spirit;* Philippians 1:11 *Being **filled** with the fruits of righteousness, which are by Jesus Christ, unto the glory and praise of God. See Appendix A.*)

The Greek word used repeatedly for "filled" is "pleroo" (Strong's #4137). Here is Strong's definition of it:

   1) to make full, to fill up, i.e. to fill to the full
      a) to cause to abound, to furnish or supply liberally
         1) I abound, I am liberally supplied
   2) to render full, i.e. to complete

a) to fill to the top: so that nothing shall be wanting to full measure, fill to the brim
b) to consummate: a number
    1) to make complete in every particular, to render perfect
    2) to carry through to the end, to accomplish, carry out, (some undertaking)
c) to carry into effect, bring to realisation, realise
    1) of matters of duty: to perform, execute
    2) of sayings, promises, prophecies, to bring to pass, ratify, accomplish
    3) to fulfil, i.e. to cause God's will (as made known in the law) to be obeyed as it should be, and God's promises (given through the prophets) to receive fulfilment

(Thayer's Lexicon also has a lot to say. Do a search for "filled" on www.BlueLetterBible.com or see Appendix B.)

The point is, Jesus wants us FULL and He knows that only HE can do it. We're all going to be full of SOMETHING. If our bodies are the temple of God and He lives in us, do you really want Him sharing space with that icky stuff? Shouldn't you be purified and cleansed of all unrighteousness so that He can reign supreme? It says "the prayers of a righteous man availeth much" - so I guess the prayers of a kind-of righteous man availeth practically nothing. Why is HE going to listen to YOU when you ask for something, when YOU won't listen to HIM about getting the red stuff out (and the stinky yellow stuff)? Proverbs 25:26 says: *"Like a muddied spring or a polluted well is a righteous man who gives way to the wicked."* That sounds to me like a cup that should be clean, but isn't.

Areas of direct disobedience or unresolved pain result in a draining off of that with which we are filled. Sometimes we have a really hard time keeping our cup full because we have a big crack in our cup caused by an unforgiveness or a bitterness or a fundamental character flaw, and so we drain out almost as soon as we get filled. Sometimes we can't ever get all the way full because of the goo we refuse to clean out that's taking up too much space in our cup. Really entrenched red stuff keeps us from being able to be filled to capacity. Sometimes there are physical oppressions and sicknesses that have resulted from spiritual problems. These, too, need addressing through the power of Jesus. More on all that later.

So, as it relates to the Body, let's start with this:

Is God telling you to do something with FOOD other than what you are doing? If yes, why won't you obey?

Is God telling you to do something with DRINK other than what you are doing? If yes, why won't you obey?

Is God telling you to do something with WORK other than what you are doing? If yes, why won't you obey?

Is God telling you to do something with MONEY other than what you are doing? If yes, why won't you obey?

Is God telling you to do something with SEX other than what you are doing? If yes, why won't you obey?

Is God telling you to do something with TIME other than what you are doing? If yes, why won't you obey?

Is God telling you to do something with your TONGUE other than what you are doing? If yes, why won't you obey?

Get the idea? Odds are pretty good that if the Holy Spirit is convicting you of something and you're not obeying, it's because you've given the enemy room in your heart or because your own soulish nature just wants to rebel. Either way, it's not really giving <u>ALL</u> and you need to do something about it. Stop thinking that He's just going to overlook it and cut you some slack. He REALLY doesn't like being in there with that stuff and He's a really big God. More fear of the Lord would be good. You might want to pray for that (like now). Crying is good, too.

If the Holy Spirit is NOT convicting you of any of that stuff, then either you are not listening and you've got a giant pride problem blocking your hearing OR the Holy Spirit has already beaten you into submission on all those levels. I've met both kinds. Just in case, now would be a good time to pray sincerely and ask the Lord to show you ANYTHING that displeases Him or any area of rebellion as it relates to your Body.

> Romans 7:17-18 – *Now then it is no more I that do it, but sin that dwelleth in me. For I know that in me (that is, in my flesh,) dwelleth no good thing: for to will is present with me; but [how] to perform that which is good I find not.*

Ok, OK!! You caught me, so what do I do about it?

Well, the first thing is to tell God you're really sorry. That would be good. He's been waiting a long time to hear that. And if you've been saying it before but then going back like a dog to his own vomit, then He's probably not going to take your apology very seriously until you start sticking by your commitments to Him.

If you've tried to turn away from stuff and haven't been able to, it's probably because you're doing too much of the fighting in your own power - because you've tried to force obedience with the YOU in your cup. That just puts more and more pressure on you and more and more guilt when you fall. Jesus lives inside of you and <u>HE</u> is not addicted to cigarettes or donuts or porn or work or anything. He doesn't worry or fear or covet or worship anything but the One True God. He has faced down every failing of Man and beaten it. If you will get out of the way and let HIM fight your battles, it will be much easier. Much. We'll cover that more later since it applies to all three of these components.

You need to be clear that SIN means "missing the mark." Whether it's murder or disbelief, it's sin and it keeps you from walking in the FULLNESS of Christ. You will not reach your maximum potential in Him if you remain unsubmitted in some areas – ANY areas. Jesus said, if you LOVE Him, you will OBEY Him. If you're not obeying Him 100%, then you must not love Him 100%. And 90% isn't going to cut it! He wants ALL – and ALL means ALL.

Soul

Let's try this same process again:

Is God telling you to do something with ANGER other than what you are doing? If yes, why won't you obey?

What about Guilt, Lust, Control, Fear, Money, Pride, Jealousy, Lying, Disbelief, Self-pity, Power, Bitterness, Unforgiveness, Gluttony, Idolatry, Rebellion or others? Got any of those?

Simplified substantially, the soul is the mind - our emotions, our mental state, our rationalizations and reactions internally to the world around us. It is what makes us distinctly us. This, too, needs to be brought fully into submission with God.

In a sense, you could see it like this:

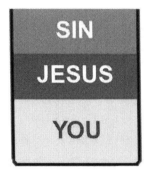

Body is where Sin manifests into the physical realm.

Our spirit is dormant until replaced with His Spirit and revived. Then it can take up the slack if we allow it to rule and reign.

Soul/Mind is where Sin begins and gets invited in. Can still be Sin even if it doesn't manifest, just by "dwelling." Our fallen nature always tries to open doors to Sin.

The yellow stuff (YOU) is our soulish nature and it's not that much better than the red stuff. In fact, the blue (JESUS) washes away all of our sins in an instant when we ask for forgiveness, but if we don't fill the gap with Jesus (and keep it full), the red bad stuff (SIN) will just jump back into the vacuum. It's our yellow stuff that invited all the red stuff! The Blood of Jesus is sufficient to heal us, but it's not the same process as with the red stuff. The Word says we're to crucify pieces of us so that Christ in us can live. We're to carry our cross daily. Well, that's about denying ourselves pleasures that might be red stuff, but it's also about watching chunks of Self die so Christ can increase and YOU can decrease. And I can tell you from LOTS of experience with this - getting the red stuff out is A LOT easier than getting all the yellow stuff out that displeases Him! One is about behavior and the other is about our nature. Habits are far easier to change than character. Beating the yellow stuff into submission is the crucifying ourselves part.

No physical trial you will ever go through - not climbing Mount Everest in winter, not sawing your own arm off with a pocket knife, not doing a marathon on your knees - will EVER be as hard as getting your tongue and your mind beaten into submission. THAT is the great battle in our lives and the difficulty is evidenced by how really rare it is to find someone that has accomplished any substantial measure of success in that! In fact, I'm convinced the only way to do it effectively is to let Jesus do it. We can fake it for awhile in our own power, but all we've done is suppress it. Only Jesus can terminate it once and for all.

In fact, it's not possible to walk in holiness at all without the Holy Spirit doing it. You can't use the yellow stuff to beat down the yellow stuff. That just won't work. Jesus is our righteousness and He alone is worthy and holy and capable of making us like Him. We can't get to be like Jesus in our own power. We have to be clothed in Christ, we have to run into Him who is our strong tower. We have to be dead so that Christ in us can live. And not just a little dead either - ALL of those component pieces have to die. Maybe this will help you figure out which is which.

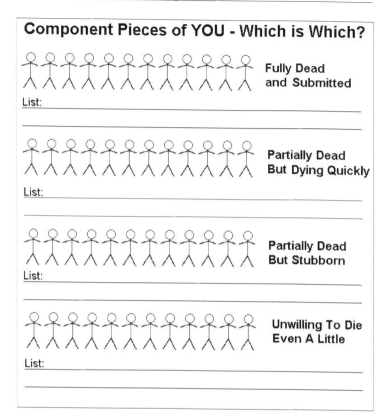

Component Pieces of YOU - Which is Which?

Fully Dead
and Submitted

List: _____

_____

Partially Dead
But Dying Quickly

List: _____

_____

Partially Dead
But Stubborn

List: _____

_____

Unwilling To Die
Even A Little

List: _____

_____

He doesn't want to purge you of ALL the yellow stuff. That would eliminate you completely and He kind of likes parts of you. Once I asked Him what parts of me He wanted to keep and He said, "Basically everything from before about six years old." Just the faith like a child parts. That thing in David that made him fearlessly go out to face Goliath because he just KNEW His Dad was bigger and tougher than THAT guy's Dad!

There's a lot more to be said, but you'll need to pray through this yourself and ask God to show you very clearly all the areas in which you are partially or completely unsubmitted. I know it's a prayer He wants you to pray, so I KNOW He will answer it and show you stuff. Then it's up to you to lay it down.

I find that this kind of prayer helps a lot and gets nearly instant results - if you have the guts to pray it:

(In case you forgot, go back and read the Warning first!)

Dear Lord, I'm really sorry for all the sin that I should have never let in. I'm sorry for all the old stuff that I've let take root and boss me around. Please purge me of all unrighteousness right now through the power of Your Blood. I stand in faith, knowing that Your Blood is sufficient to cleanse me of all unrighteousness. Please show me ANY area of my life that displeases You – anything that stands in the way between us and keeps me from being able to walk in the fulness of all that you have for me. Whatever it is, I don't care how much I like it, I don't care how long it's been there, I don't care how much it hurts, it's got to go RIGHT NOW in the Name of Jesus. So Lord, rip it, tear it, burn it, shred it, crucify it – whatever it takes. If I won't lay it down, rip it from my grasp. I don't care how much it hurts, I trust You. Do whatever it takes, but do it RIGHT NOW. I won't flinch and I won't try to hop out of Your refining fire when it comes. Dial the heat up. I'm going to stand. Give me the strength to stand. Please hold my hand. I'm going to really need You. Thanks, Lord. You're the best Dad ever and I trust You. Please burn it all off and don't stop no matter how much I whine. In the Name of Jesus, Amen.

Hear me – your growth in Christ is <u>directly</u> <u>proportional</u> to your willingness to rush headlong into the refining fire and give it a wet, sloppy kiss. When He is pounding on you and life seems horrible, if you will go to Him and find out what He's trying to teach you, embrace it, learn from it and thank Him for it - then maybe you can move on. If you whine and complain and keep asking Him to turn down the flames because it's too hot, it shows a lack of trust that He knows what He's doing and it just slows down the whole process. How long is it going to take to cook a turkey in an oven set at 100 degrees? How long if it's set at 450? That's the difference between Christians in China and India and those in America. We have our ovens set at 100 degrees and they have theirs on full blast. Persecution dials up the heat really fast – and results in explosive growth in Christ (and a sifting of those who mean it and those who don't).

So don't be such a sissy. Jump in the fire and learn to like it. Is He God or isn't He? Will He protect you or won't He? Are His promises good or aren't they? Buck up, ya big weenie. Go kill some yellow stuff.

Spirit

OK, so we got the red stuff out (for today) and we begged Him to kill the yellow stuff. So you probably have a void in the top of your cup now. What are you going to do? If you leave it like that the enemy, who ranges to and fro like a hungry lion, will try to jump in there right away and mess with you again. You've got to get your cup full of Jesus and keep it that way.

And not just full to 100%, full to overflowing – up and over, mounded up on top.

So do you know how? Well, you can read your Bible. You can listen to worship music. You can pray. You can just spend time at the feet of Jesus – like Mary. Whatever is the best way you have found to drink in Jesus. But be careful that you're not DOING to get filled – like Martha. That just means that you're trying to get more blue stuff by engaging the yellow stuff. That's a long uphill battle toward legalism. You can't earn the Holy Spirit. What it ends up doing is inviting in the red stuff again in the form of guilt, condemnation, self-righteousness, pride or some other nasty thing.

Maybe there's a better way. What does the Word of God say about this?

John 7:38 says: *"He who believes in Me, as the Scripture said, 'From his innermost being will flow rivers of living water.'"*

John 4:10 says: *"Jesus answered and said unto her, If thou knewest the gift of God, and who it is that saith to thee, Give me to drink; thou wouldest have asked of him, and he would have given thee living water."*

Rev. 7:17 says: *"For the Lamb which is in the midst of the throne shall feed them, and shall lead them unto living fountains of waters: and God shall wipe away all tears from their eyes."*

Here's a couple of Old Testament reference so you know God doesn't change:

Jeremiah 17:13 – *O LORD, the hope of Israel, all that forsake thee shall be ashamed, [and] they that depart from me shall be written in the earth, because they have forsaken the LORD, the fountain of living waters.*

Jeremiah 2:13 – *For my people have committed two evils; they have forsaken me the fountain of living waters, [and] hewed them out cisterns, broken cisterns, that can hold no water.*

In that last one we see that they committed two evils, they didn't drink of the living waters and they had containers with cracks in them. (A cistern is just a really big cup.) In fact, they made their own cisterns to store up water because they didn't trust in God's unending supply from the fountain. And the result was that they had neither – AND they made God mad!

It sure seems to me like those fountains of living water are the Holy Spirit. It says Jesus is the "Fountain in the House of David" (Zech 13:1) The Holy Spirit is that blue stuff that fills us and displaces all the other stuff. It would be great if He would just shove everything out of the way, but for some reason we're involved and we have to participate in the process – or at least be willing and ask Him to do it.

This being true (I hope you agree), then we don't need to DO anything to fill our cup. We just have to believe that Jesus wants our cup full, that He promised that springs of living water would flow up from INSIDE of us – and then just turn on the tap. We just need to ask Him to fill us in whatever way HE wants to fill us and teach us how to keep it that way. Remember; trust the Lord your God with ALL your heart, lean NOT on your OWN understanding, but in ALL your ways acknowledge HIM and HE will direct your paths. (Prov. 3:5-6)

I think our job as a church is to find those who are poor in spirit – those whose cups are running low – and share with them. Pour ourselves out into them so that they can be filled. Not with our yellow stuff! God forbid! But from the abundance of the riches that have been given to us that we would share – of our wealth, of our physical energy, strength, time AND of the fountain of living water that is inside of us.

Haven't you ever been around somebody that, just being in the same room with them or getting a hug, made your spirit feel full? I bet they had a cup that was overflowing – or they deliberately and selflessly poured themselves out on you. They may not have known that's what they were doing or been able to explain it that way, they just knew that they had Joy and Peace and that you needed some, so they shared.

Go back and look again at the picture of the pyramid of champagne glasses where they pour in the top one and as it overflows, the glass below gets filled and overflows and so it continues all the way down. Those who have the biggest cup of Jesus should be constantly pouring themselves out onto others and teaching them how to keep it going.

Shouldn't church be a filling station? How often do you go and leave feeling just as empty as when you got there? Some churches are really great filling stations and you can leave FULL of Jesus – but you can't make it past Monday afternoon without running out again. That's because we think we have to go to a building to get our cups full. The Word of God doesn't say anything like that. The Word of God says rivers of living water will flow up from INSIDE of us. We have an endless supply at our disposal all the time! And WE are supposed to be the filling station for those that don't know how to tap into it. It's not about the building or the pastor or nice music that gets us in the mood – every Christian has access to the river of God! Isn't that COOL!! So, stick a straw in and suck! Better yet, just dive in! The better you see in the spirit, the easier it will be for you to get a handle on this. I'm not talking about theory here, this is totally real to those that understand the things of the Spirit and ignore the things of this world. Faith is the key that opens the door. Believe like a child that God's promises are good and that He means what He says. Then just reach out and grab it.

Later we're going to talk more about all the things you can be filled with, why you need to help fill others and how to get full and make sure you stay full. I know this may sound weird, but it's all in the Bible. No question about it. We're supposed to perceive things in the spirit, not with our natural mind. This earth is NOT the "real" world – this is not our home. We are spiritual beings and we need to get a lot more familiar with what's happening in the spirit. That's where the war is and that's where our hope comes from.

> I Corinthians 2:14 – *But the natural man receiveth not the things of the Spirit of God: for they are foolishness unto him: neither can he know them, because they are* **spiritually** *discerned.*

> Romans 8:6 – *For to be carnally minded [is] death; but to be* **spiritually minded** *is life and peace.*

COMMUNICATIONS –
HOTLINE TO HEADQUARTERS

Why do we need to do this? Because you need to hear REALLY clearly from Headquarters before we start passing out new weapons you don't know what to do with! The last thing we need is more friendly fire accidents when you go firing off stuff like Prophecy or Tongues without having been trained. You could do some serious damage – trust me. It's really important that we get your pipeline all cleaned out so that you know what to give, what to ask for, and what to do with it. If there is stuff in the way, we need to get it out so your motives will be right and He can call the shots.

OK, so we got the red stuff out, we're getting more yellow stuff out, we learned how to get more blue stuff, now what? Well, now it's time to get your filters unclogged so you can hear God really well and HE can direct ALL your paths. This works better as a question and answer thing. Ready?

First, what exactly are we talking about? Does God really speak to people today?

Yes. In a whole bunch of ways from a gentle nudge, to instruction through the Word, to using other people and circumstances to speak to you, to sending dreams and visions (or angels) – and/or even conversing directly with you.

You can hear God and converse with Him?! You're kidding, right?

Not kidding. You can absolutely talk to God and He'll talk back. There are millions of people all over the world that rely on God for constant daily instruction on all sorts of things. But, there's a difference between hearing God audibly (with your natural ears, outside of your own head) and hearing the inner "still, small voice". It's pretty rare for God to speak to people audibly (like thunder), but there are plenty of folks out there that say they've heard Him – and the evidence is that once they did, it changed them forever!

Many of the house churches in China are under such persecution that they can't set a regular time for meeting or even tell each other when the meeting will be – they all just pray independently and God Himself sets the time and place and tells each to be there. I've experienced that kind of coordination myself and hear Him speak to me all the time. This is totally for real and the birthright of every believer! He's your Dad and He wants to talk to you.

Wait ... people hear the God of the Universe tell them stuff? Like what tie to wear and whether to turn left or right? What job to take? What to have for dinner? Not just big stuff?

Sure. The Bible says, "In all your ways acknowledge Him and He will direct your paths." (Prov. 3:5-6) What do you think

"ALL your ways" means? And how is He going to direct you if you can't hear Him?

But my pastor said God doesn't talk to people like that!

Hmmm. Well, God used to talk to people all the time in the Bible. Wonder when He stopped? Did He say He was going to stop? Isn't He the same yesterday, today and forever? If anything, once the Holy Spirit came in Acts 2, there were LOTS MORE people talking to God directly! Never mind the MILLIONS of people all over the world who you have to conclude are thoroughly and certifiably nuts – including many of the most effective leaders of the church. In order to sustain that argument you have all kinds of logic problems.

Consider this;

IF God used to talk to people but doesn't now, **THEN** we must not need to hear from Him anymore. Can that be? By all measures we're worse off than ever. If there is a war between Good and Evil, we're losing pretty badly right now and really desperately need to be getting commands directly from Headquarters, not from flawed man-made sources and tradition-soaked interpretations of Scripture!

IF there is a battle between Good and Evil, **THEN** who would benefit most if the people on the "Good" side were told they couldn't ACTUALLY talk to their Commander in Chief? Now, you know the "Evil" side is absolutely clear to EVERYONE that if you try to talk to THEIR leadership you WILL get an answer REAL fast! Even Christians are afraid to mess with Ouija boards and call on the names of demons because somewhere inside they believe something VERY real will show up almost instantly. But at the same time, the forces of darkness want us to buy that OUR God is mute! Doesn't that sound like something the snake would say in the Garden? Despite hundreds of examples in the Bible that He is available and accessible all the time, we have too often bought the lie that God is unwilling or unable to actually talk to His children. It's a lie from the pit and we've bought into it for too long.

IF we receive the Holy Spirit when we are saved, **THEN** 1/3 of the Godhead is living INSIDE of us all the time! (I John 4:13-17) But He doesn't have anything to say?! He's not interested in our daily activities? God's not big enough to know what we should have for lunch? He knows the hairs on our head and monitors our every coming and going, but has no opinion about it or desire to give us advice? What kind of Father is that?! **IF** we're dead and it's Christ in us that lives, **THEN** shouldn't HE be running the show? (Romans 7:4-6)

The most common argument I hear is that when the Bible was done being written then "that which was perfect has come and that which was in part was done away" (I Corin. 13:10) so we don't need to talk to God anymore. The argument is that I Corinthians 12 talks about tongues and prophecy and then chapter 13 tells about the way it SHOULD be when the perfect is come so you should do away with all that. But they don't seem to notice that then chapter 14 starts with Paul urging them to seek the gift of prophecy! Said another way, I think "when that which is perfect is come" refers to Jesus returning, NOT the Bible being completed.

IF the Bible is what's being referred to there, **THEN** why hasn't knowledge ceased? **IF** it's the "perfect" thing mentioned there, **THEN** nothing could stand against it. **IF** the Bible is perfect, **THEN** could somebody tell me which version is flawless? And **IF** none of them are because we don't have the original manuscripts anymore, **THEN** something DID stand against it! **IF** the perfect is come, **THEN** why do we have 37,000+ denominations and we seem to be losing the battle with the darkness? There are just big giant logic problems with that argument – not to mention the personal experience of millions of reasonable, Jesus-lovers all over the world.

But my pastor says that even HE doesn't hear God conversationally like that!

Ok, well, you see, Matthew 18:18 says that, "what you bind on earth will be bound in heaven and what you loose on earth will be loosed in heaven." It goes on to say that if two of you on earth agree about anything you ask for, it will be done for you by the Father in heaven. (v. 19) So, could it be that we have whole groups of Christians that have agreed that God doesn't talk to people? And if they were convinced of that, don't those verses say that God will honor it? So maybe the problem is that if you're convinced God WON'T talk to you that way, He probably won't. And who would you blame? The pastor? Probably not – in fairness, we gotta lay it at the feet of the snake and the generations of tradition that have been built up to keep us from being truly "Spirit-led".

There could also be other problems that would keep a person from hearing God. One possibility is that you're on the wrong team - even if you think you're not. You know it's possible to make up your own "Jesus" and you'll get a response from that one about as good as if you were praying to a stick of wood. Another is that you have unrepented sin that stands between you and God – and God has convicted you of it so many times that He's just given up trying to talk to you about it.

Oh, and by the way, you're going to have to get over that thing about the pastor being more "holy" than you. This is a one-on-

one relationship with Jesus you're supposed to have. You can't do it by proxy through the guy that gets paid to hear God (especially if he admits he's NOT hearing God!). We are ALL the Church. We are EACH temples that hold God's Spirit. Any one of us that are adopted sons of God have the ability to petition the Throne directly and seek His face. God loves each – in fact, He's especially fond of those that come to Him with faith like little children. Sometimes pastors have a hard time with that. (I don't think there are "Faith like a Child" classes in seminary.)

This is just crazy! How could this be true and I never knew it before? Wouldn't somebody have told me?

Well, I think you underestimate the damage the enemy has done and how long he's been plotting this. The vast majority of the church in the West doesn't live the "normal" Christian life. That is, Biblically speaking, we're to be full of power and might, we're to be free of the bondage of sin, we're to NOT conform to the world, we're to be dead to ourselves, we're to be ONE Body and loving and serving each other with all our heart. That's just a few. Can you see how far away from that we actually are as a "church"? We're not even CLOSE! There MUST be something missing. Somebody left something out! It has to be this – God Himself is supposed to be directing you and you're supposed to be listening and OBEYING. Now ... who would benefit most from us leaving that little piece out? Yep, the guy in the black hat.

Now, what do you think a close encounter conversationally with the God of the Universe might do to a person? Trust me, it would change everything. It would show them the power of the relationship they have as adopted sons, they would lose all fear, they would sacrifice anything to keep hearing Him, they would obey and walk in HIS ways, they would know (really KNOW) that God Himself lives IN them and they would want more of Him, they would do the things on HIS heart – like feeding the hungry, clothing the naked, saving the lost. They would be in awe of His holiness and seek to please Him out of reverence and honor, not out of legalism or church requirements.

So, **IF** this is a war between Good and Evil, **THEN** wouldn't our most immediate and urgent need be to get people to where they can hear clear, timely, reliable commands from Headquarters? If you have a guy in Basic Training that refuses to listen to the Drill Sergeant and does his own thing, wouldn't you want to leave him at home? He's just going to get himself killed when the enemy starts shooting and leadership says 'DUCK!' and he can't or won't hear them! He's no good to anybody. Maybe he could be a supply clerk – but he really shouldn't be on the front lines. He should stay home and send his money to the folks on the front lines that hear God really well and obey ALL the time, no matter what the cost.

But we have the Bible. God's Word is what we are to use to direct our paths!

Ok, sure. Not got anything bad to say about the Bible! Everything God tells us to do will line up with His own Word. But no matter how well you know the Bible, it can't accommodate for every possible situation and what you should do. There's lots of stuff not covered in there – like which of these two jobs God wants me to take. And there's stuff in there that men have been arguing about for centuries without ever getting agreement. Lots of wasted time trying to figure out how many angels can dance on the head of a pin. (By the way, which side benefits most when God's people fight over stupid stuff? You getting the hang of this yet?)

Think of it like this. You're in the Army and they give you a Manual. All kinds of stuff is covered in there – what to wear, how to salute, how the weapons work, how to survive in a battle, what to eat in the forest, how the chain of command works, even what the enemy is like and how to resist them – there's even stuff in there about what the enemy WILL DO one day, whether they like it or not! It's a REALLY good Manual – in fact, it's inspired by God! It covers an amazing array of stuff and could probably handle most any situation. So would the Drill Sergeant ask you to read it, maybe even memorize it – and then send you into battle with nothing BUT that? Are you going to be able to know what to do when the bullets start flying? What about group strategy and deployment of forces and anticipating enemy movements? Is the Manual going to accommodate for every possible scenario on a rapidly changing battlefield? Are you sure you're interpreting it right? Is there time in the foxhole to be arguing with other soldiers that are reading it differently? What if some idiot published like TWENTY different translations and paraphrases of the Manual?! Then what?! Are you REALLY sure you have the right version? Isn't there a chain of command? Isn't there somebody in charge calling the shots that's supposed to tell you what to do next? Aren't you supposed to be listening and OBEYING? Want to go into battle without the Manual? No. Want to rely on it alone when you have other resources available? No. Want to take an order from somebody that goes against the Manual? No. When the bullets start flying, do you want to hear personally and directly from Headquarters so that you can know that help is coming and know what to do? You betcha!

We need a radio to headquarters that works really good, with no static on the line and no enemy transmissions sneaking in. If you insist that you don't want to hear God, I still love you, but I'm not going to the front lines with you.

I don't know. This is kind of scary. What if I hear wrong? What if it's the enemy messing with me? Maybe this is all in your mind.

Wow! That's a whole mess of stuff. Let's try this one at a time.

Maybe it's all in your mind.

Well, it's not just me. There's hundreds of millions like me that hear God. In fact, most of the growth in the Church worldwide is because of those people. The "mainline" denominations are shrinking. It's the Spirit-led revolutionaries that are exploding into new territories and pushing back the darkness. The growth in this arm of the Church went from about ZERO in 1900 to about 500 MILLION people in 2000. God is pouring out His Spirit and people are listening.

Ok, let's try it from the opposite direction. It all sunk in for me one day when it struck me that satan never creates anything – he just makes weak copies of whatever God is doing. He's a liar and a deceiver and a fake. So ... while it may seem far-fetched, most folks (even Christians) will admit that evil is a real force in the world and the supernatural is real. (The Bible verifies repeatedly that witches and mediums and sorcery are real, by the way ... and that you're headed for hell if you mess with them. – Deuteronomy 18:10-12, Colossians. 5:20) The enemy has psychics and mediums and astral-projection and Ouija boards and demons and zombies and spells and curses.

So where's OUR stuff?! If this is a war, why does only one side get cool weapons? Was my church leaving out important stuff that I needed for warfare? Because in the first century they had amazing weapons and defenses available to them. They had the Holy Spirit telling them stuff they wouldn't have known (Acts 5:1-11), they had people hearing from God (Acts 13:2), they had people writing stuff as God dictated (Rev.), they were caught up in the Spirit to heaven (2 Corin. 12:2-4), they had dreams and visions (Acts 10:9-23), they saw angels (Acts 12), they saw Jesus Himself (Acts 9:1-22), they cast out demons (Acts 16:16-18), they were bitten by deadly snakes and didn't die (Acts 28:1-10), they spoke in other languages of men and of angels (Acts 2, I Corin. 12 & more), they healed people (Acts 5:15), they prayed and miracles happened (Acts 5:12, Acts 12) – even teleportation (or as I prefer "theoportation" - Acts 8:39) and they raised the dead (Acts 9:32-42)! They even had people who were against them drop dead (Acts 5:1-11) or go blind (Acts 13:6-12) – on command! And that's just ONE reference for each! There are lots more!

Now, the argument is that all that ended when the Bible was done being written – but it didn't end for the other team, so how come just all OUR cool stuff got taken away? Wouldn't it have really benefited the enemy a LOT to spread around that story that we were powerless – for a couple thousand years? Do you see? This is no kind of way to fight a war! There MUST be stuff we've been leaving out! The enemy has us twisted up into a thousand pieces (41,000+ denominations to be specific) and we can't STAND because we're not ONE Body. Because of all the arguing over stupid stuff – which we would NEVER have done if we had all been hearing the voice of God personally and reliably and walking in the Gifts!

This is kind of scary.

No kidding! It's the biggest thing ever in your life! That the God of the Universe wants to be intimately involved in everything you do and say and eat and wear and think. That's massively scary! And yet, we can never have peace and joy and victory until we have relationship with Jesus and are led by His Holy Spirit. You see, under our own power, we just screw everything up. There has never been any strategy of Man that has led to anything good in the long run. Oh, it might work for a little while, but you get enough sinful people involved in it, add money, mix in a little satan – and it's toast. Or worse, you get Communism or Fascism or something and millions of people die. There are just two options – if it's of Man it will fail and if it's of God nothing can stand against it. (Acts 5:38-39) Since the "church" in America is failing, somebody other than God must be in charge. See a logic problem there?

Anyway, yes, it's scary. But what a payoff!! To walk in holiness because God Himself is fighting off the temptations and snares of the enemy, to hear Him all the time and get direction on anything and everything, to know that He is completely and totally in charge at all times in every situation. How are you going to find peace WITHOUT hearing from God? How is what you have NOW working for you?

And hearing His voice is not even a GIFT of the Spirit! It's just an automatic for every believer! We haven't even talked about prophecy and discernment of spirits and knowledge and wisdom and tongues and healing and all the other gifts God gives His children! Trust me, the payoff is amazing, but it's going to cost you everything – but everything you THINK you have isn't yours anyway, so who cares!?

What if I hear wrong? What if the enemy is messing with me?

Well sure, that can happen. He's certainly going to try to confuse and frustrate you. We are specifically instructed, "do not believe every spirit, but test the spirits to see whether they are from God (1 John 4:1). That MUST mean that other spirits are potentially messing with us, and since there is no indication that THIS ended when the Bible was completed, then there must still be demons putting thoughts into our heads. And if there are still demons putting thoughts into our heads, then we must still have a need to test and see if they are from God. And if they're NOT from God, then we resist them and they flee. But it must also mean that one of the possibilities is that the spirit we're hearing IS from God! (Again, proving the point that God still speaks to us despite I Corin. 13:10.)

You see 1 John 4 goes on in verses 2 and 3 to lay out how you can know what it is that is talking to you and from where it comes, "This is how you can recognize the Spirit of God: Every spirit that acknowledges that Jesus Christ has come in the flesh is from God, but every spirit that does not acknowledge Jesus is not from God. This is the spirit of the antichrist, which you have heard is coming and even now is already in the world."

When we get a thought in our head we have to figure out who it is. There are only three choices: You, God or the enemy. Sometimes other people tell us stuff, but they're still playing to one of the three. We're to bring every thought into obedience with Christ (and the Word). That means our own thoughts that are out of line AND the ones inserted by the enemy. I find that, sadly, the enemy and I sound a lot alike. The red stuff and the yellow stuff aren't really that different after all. I apply this filter to everything, "If I follow through with this thought that just came into my head, who is glorified most – God, satan or me?" If it's anything other than God, even if it's me, I rebuke in the Name of Jesus. And if it WAS me, I ask the Lord to hunt down whatever in me wanted to suggest something that wouldn't glorify Him – and kill it.

Could you screw it up? Sure. Particularly if the voices are VERY sneaky. Which they <u>will</u> be because demons are smarter than us and know the human condition very well after all these years of torturing and twisting us. Without God fighting for you, you haven't got a chance. You have to be constantly on guard, constantly armored-up and expecting anything from any direction. But His arm is long and His shields are mighty. He will always get you through if you are sincerely seeking Him and trying to walk in holiness.

OK. I'm getting that it's possible, but I'm going to have to hear Him for myself. I'm willing to try. What do we do?

Great! Yeah, don't take my word for it, seek Him yourself. Well the first thing is to ask the Lord to show you anything that stands in the way between you and Him.

It's like this:

There is a pipeline of information that flows between us and God. He ALWAYS hears us, but if we can't hear Him, it's probably because of things WE have put in the way.

ANYTHING that we put between US and GOD is an idol. God never puts those things there, WE do. The most common thing is "religion" or the "pastor." Then ALL messages from God have to filter THROUGH that and get garbled. Others include sins and habits and addictions and disobedience of one sort or another.

They ALL have to go. Only THEN can we get clear commands from Upstairs. Don't let ANYTHING come between You and God.

The point of the church coming together should be so that we can crucify pieces of ourselves so that Christ in us can live. Said another way, it's to help each other identify the things that stand between us and Jesus – and pluck them out.

The most common thing we put in the way is our belief that God won't talk to us. That's got to go! If you don't think He's a Living God and active and able to speak and desiring relationship with you, then you're going to have to lay that down.

One of the other possibilities is that you're worshiping the WRONG Jesus. Paul said that would happen, that someone would come preaching another Jesus and people would accept it. It's very simple; if you make up your own Jesus, don't expect an answer when you pray! Prosperity-Jesus, Emergency-Only-Jesus, Not-Quite-As-Good-As-The-Virgin-Mary-Jesus, and a zillion others are all MADE UP. If you make your own god from scratch, expect about as much response as if you were praying to a stick. Those are NOT Bible Jesus - who doesn't like to be toyed with and put in a box.

Other things in the way are a reliance on someone else for your holiness or connection to God (Pastor, wife, mother, etc.). That's got to stop. This is a ONE-on-ONE relationship with Jesus. Nobody is going to do it for you. Other pipeline blockages include addiction, pride, selfishness, bitterness, anger, laziness, fear and so many others that keep us from experiencing the fullness that is IN Christ.

Ask the Lord to show you what is in the way and He is faithful to ALWAYS do that if you'll listen. Ask some other folks to pray with you if possible and just pray in agreement that the Lord will make Himself very clear to you about what to do next.

Just pray and believe. He'll come and help unclog you. Believe that He wants to talk to you and start conversing with Him. Find someone to be accountable with that knows God really well and make sure you don't act on anything that sounds fishy without verifying it with the Word of God. Now, not with doctrine of Man, mind you – with the Word of God.

If you like, pray something like this:

> *Lord, I'm sorry I ever put you in a box. I'm sorry I limited You in any way. I'm sorry that I haven't been hearing you as well as I should and I acknowledge that I clogged up my pipeline with stuff. Please, Lord, whatever it takes,*

scrub it all out of there with the Blood of Jesus. I just want You, Jesus. You direct my paths and organize my days. You tell me what You want and I'll do it. Help me hear You better. Help make me dangerous to the enemy. Increase the Jesus in me, even if it hurts. I love you, Lord. You be in charge now. Amen.

DOES GOD STILL SPEAK TO
PEOPLE TODAY?

Posted by EttyB on the F.O.T.M. online discussion board.

Some years ago, I had awakened before my family and I was in the kitchen when I heard the voice of the Lord say, "Roast a chicken." I had heard His voice before, so I said, "I'll be glad to, Lord, if You will tell me who to give it to." While I was speaking, I was pulling a chicken from my freezer and preparing to thaw it.

"I want you to take it to Mrs. Ming." He said.

I didn't know Mrs. Ming. I knew of her, though. I knew that she was an elderly woman in our church who was the wife of a retired minister. I knew that she had cancer and that her elderly husband was caring for her. I didn't know what she looked like, had never spoken to her, and didn't know where they lived.

But, the Lord had spoken, so I thawed the chicken and prepared it for roasting, then put it in the oven. As I prepared it, I thought of other things I might fix to make a complete meal. Fluffy fruit salad...mashed potatoes and gravy, corn. It sounded good, even to me!

It was just a few minutes before noon when the meal was ready and I decided that I would call our church office and see if anyone knew the address of the Mings. It was Saturday and I knew the office was closed, but I called anyway. Someone answered the phone and gave me the address of the elderly couple. Bless them!

I got a large box, armed with the address, and headed out to a nearby town that I was not familiar with. Within two minutes of driving into the town I was at their house!

Still, I felt rather foolish pulling into the driveway of complete strangers, holding a big cardboard box and saying, "Hey, I'm here with a chicken dinner that God told me to bring to you!" That was out of my comfort zone!

But...I got the box out of the back of my car and did just that. A little man with a dear face opened the door and looked at me questioningly. "Yes?" he said.

"God told me to bring you a chicken dinner for lunch, so here I am. Have you already eaten?"

He opened the door and stepped aside, motioning me to set the box on the kitchen counter. I lifted the hot dishes out of the box and took the covers off.

Not only had they not eaten. The kitchen was dark and nothing had even been started in the way of a meal. The little man looked jolly as he said they hadn't had a bite.

He lovingly prepared a plate for his sick wife and took it in to her darkened room. "This lady has brought us a roasted chicken for lunch," he told her. I was still in the kitchen when he came back and said, "My wife would like to talk to you."

I walked into the room of a woman who was in the last stages of cancer. She reached a frail hand out to me and in a soft voice she said, "This morning, I was so hungry for chicken I thought I couldn't stand it! So, I said, 'Jesus, I don't know how You can do it or if You even think it's important enough, but if You could get me some roasted chicken, I would be SO happy!" She looked at me with the sweetest expression and said, "He used you!"

That dear lady went home to be with Jesus before the next week was out and the Lord let me be His hand reaching out in love to her! What a privilege!

Later I was telling the little incident to one of my young daughter's friends and she said, "Oh, that was my grandma! She didn't have any appetite at all for weeks before she died. How nice that the Lord gave her such a blessing right before she went Home!" I thought then that if I'd failed to respond to God's voice, refused to move out of my comfort zone, that the Lord would probably have found someone else who would be faithful. But what a blessing I would have missed!

EttyB – 4/4/05

LET ME SHOW YOU A HIGHER WAY
– THE **BIG** PRAYER

First, let's pray.

> **Father God, You are worthy of glory and honor and praise. You are above all and we honor You. There is none above You, Lord. Thank You for Your son, Jesus, and for His sacrifice on our behalf. Please teach us in this time and keep us safe from anything that the enemy might try to distract us or get our eyes off of You. We love You and we praise Your Holy Name. We ask You for all of these things in the Name of our Lord Jesus Christ. Cover us in the Blood of Jesus and protect our bodies, souls and spirits from the assault of the enemy. Give us pure hearts and teach us to fear You so that we may have wisdom. Amen.**

OK, two things that need to be PERFECTLY clear about this writing and everything that we're saying here:

First, God the Father is supreme. The Holy Spirit is the conduit by which we reach the Lord Jesus Christ. Jesus is the conduit by which we reach the Almighty God and Father of All. The Holy Spirit does NOT want to be worshiped. Jesus does not want your worship. He came that the FATHER might be glorified. We love Jesus Christ and adore Him for His sacrifice and stand in awe of His love for us and willingness to endure, even now, for stinkers like us. But He came so that we might know the Father. When we talk about Fear of the Lord, we're not talking about fear of the Holy Spirit – or fear of Jesus alone. We're talking about trembling and awe of God the Father. Jesus is separate from the Father and doesn't know all that the Father knows. Even now His role is distinct and Jesus is secondary to the Father. Our worship should be for Yahweh alone. Since Jesus only says and does what the Father tells Him – and the Holy Spirit only repeats what He's told – if we obey Jesus (through the Holy Spirit), then we are obeying the Father.

So much error comes into the "church" because people are worshiping the wrong "Jesus." Some places worship the Holy Spirit and just seek manifestations. The Holy Spirit DID NOT come to be worshiped! Hear me, if you make the Holy Spirit the object of your worship, something ELSE will show up. He might be there doing stuff in the people with pure hearts, but those just seeking a "buzz" or an "experience" will get one from some other source. God judges the heart. If you come before Him seeking communion with Him but you have an impure motive, there will be curses on your head. He will lift His hand and something nasty will come as an angel of light and twist you into a pretzel.

Some people worship Jesus only. In fact, most places are

worshiping Jesus. That's exactly what the enemy wants. If he can't talk us into worshiping a tree or a rock, he'll just get us worshiping ANYTHING other then God Almighty. If we worship our ministry, our new building, our pastor, or even the Holy Spirit or Jesus – we are guilty of idolatry. The first and greatest commandment (confirmed by Jesus Himself in three of the Gospels) is this: **"Hear O Israel, the Lord your God, the Lord is one. Love the Lord your God with all your heart and with all your soul and with all your mind and with all your strength."** The Father has not backed off from that and neither has the Son. DO NOT make the mistake of letting the enemy take your eyes off of that explicit command!

We're to love, honor and adore Jesus. We're to obey Jesus. We're to abide in Jesus. But we have peace in God THROUGH our Lord Jesus Christ (Rom. 5:1) So we implore you on Christ's behalf, be reconciled to God. (2 Corin. 5:20)

When King David said, "The Lord said to my Lord," he was referencing God the Father talking to Jesus Christ. Both were "Lords" over David, even though he was the king of Israel. When we use the word "Lord" we need to be clear about which one we are talking about and what exactly "Lord" means. A Lord is a monarch, a ruler, a clear authority figure for whom you have respect. They are not an elected official. It is not a term of courtesy, like "Sir." It is not a term of endearment, like "Dad". It is not a personal name, like "Jesus". It is a title and an office and deserves respect. When you say it, you should be using it in the sense that you recognize that the one to whom you are speaking is Commander, Master, King, Ruler, Autocrat and Monarch over you. There is no middle ground, there is no other way of meaning it that isn't demeaning and insulting to the holder of the title.

If you meet with the President of the United States, you call him "Mr. President." If you're a dear friend or a relative, in some settings it may be fine to call him by his first name or a nickname. But when you come to him within the scope of his office and his authority petitioning for some favor or seeking some directive, you address him with respect and you call him "Mr. President." If you endlessly call him "Mr. President" at the beginning and the end of every sentence when you're talking to him, he's just going to think you're either nuts or you're trivializing his office and title. When you pray, don't use God's name (or title) in vain. It has power, speak it forth with respect and with a purpose, not just to fill space in a sentence or as a pause while you figure out what to say next.

Why is all this so important? Because I believe that what this teaching is all about is something so big and so radically different than what we have been doing – and so dangerous to the forces of darkness – that it's just CRITICALLY important that we make sure that everyone has a pure heart and a proper perspective before getting too far into this. The enemy is going to try every way possible to tangle this all up and to make it about ANYTHING other than God.

Second, we know from Scripture, and from past history in the Church, that when the Holy Spirit shows up and starts doing cool stuff, it's just REALLY likely that somebody is going to start trying to bottle it and sell it and make it about THEM. Plus there will be fakes and liars and counterfeits and demons dressed as angels of light. Then everyone else will look at the squirrelly mess and overreact and want to deny that ANY of it is real. We are entering into an era of MAXIMUM deception, of false signs and wonders and fake prophets. We need to be VERY careful and we need to not get sucked in by any of it or allow ourselves to drift off course and find that we're helping the cause of darkness.

How can we be sure that we stay on course? Keep our eyes on God, pray for more Fear of the Lord, obey Him at all times, walk in holiness and do everything out of Love. They will know us by our Love. By our love for the brethren and our willingness to share and sacrifice on their behalf, by our love for God and constant obedience, by our love for Jesus Christ and a willingness to sacrifice even as He sacrificed for us.

If you seek Gifts for ANY reason other than so that you can be more like Jesus and a better warrior for the armies of God, then you better think twice. In fact, pray for more Fear of the Lord and wisdom. If someone comes to you offering something, you need to hear God well enough to know who they are and IF you're to receive from them. If you have an urge to impart something to someone, you need to hear God well enough to know that it's His will and timing. You need to hear God well enough to know what to pray and how.

Let me simplify. What this is about is sacrificially pouring ourselves out onto another person. By sacrificially, I mean, even if you don't get it back. If you have a big healing ministry and it's going great and God is moving and He clearly asks you to take every gift, every anointing, every promise He's ever made to you, every expectation and hope that you have and give it all away to the twelve year old kid that just walked down the aisle – YOU DO IT! Or sit down and shut up. If you're not willing to lay down everything you have, in the physical and in the spiritual, when God directs you to, then you can't follow Him and you're not fit for the Kingdom. (Luke 9:62)

What we're aiming for here is MAXIMUM love. Something beyond what most anybody is teaching lately. I asked the Lord to teach me how to pray and He led me to Moses and Paul.

> Exodus 32:31-32 – *So Moses went back to the Lord and said, "Oh, what a great sin these people have committed! They have made themselves gods of gold. But now, please forgive their sin – but if not, then blot me out of the book you have written."*

> Romans 9:2-3 – *I have great sorrow and unceasing anguish in my heart. For I could wish that I myself were cursed and cut off from Christ for the sake of my brothers, those of my own race, the people of Israel.*

Do you get that? Jesus said:

> John 15:13 – *"Greater love has no man than this, that he lay down his life for his friends."*

What life do you think He is talking about? Which is more valuable, your physical life or your eternal life? Moses and Paul offered to be blotted out of the Book of Life if only God would hear their prayers! That prayer is so much like Jesus, God HAS to hear it. Everything in heaven stops when someone sincerely and wholeheartedly prays THAT prayer! Here are examples of two people that stood in the gap for a whole nation, a whole race and laid down the best and biggest thing they had – their eternal inheritance as sons of God. Your physical life is like a blade of grass or a flower that withers. It's nothing in the scope of things. It's a really loving thing to take a bullet for someone or run into a burning building, please don't think I'm demeaning anyone that makes that kind of sacrifice! But even though we call it that, it's not really the "ultimate" sacrifice. To offer to lay down your eternal salvation is the ultimate.

I don't want there to be any misunderstanding about where we're headed here. My goal is to get you SO full of Jesus that you can pray the really BIG prayer and mean it. My goal is to raise up an army of people that know how to lay down everything. My goal is to raise up people that will lay down everything all the time and love nothing more than obedience to God. If the Lord asks you to offer up everything so that the bunion on a sweet old lady's toe will be healed, you do it. If He asks you to lay down everything so that another could take your place and be greater than you, you do it without thinking. That's where we're headed. If you get enough Jesus in you, it's not as hard as you might think. But a love on that kind of a scale is not "normal" and requires far more than we can even imagine. If even a few of the people of God started praying like that, it would turn everything on it's ear! Heaven would open wide and His Spirit would pour out through us on all flesh.

People are going to argue that you can't lose your salvation. Whether you can or you can't, it should be clear that we have multiple Biblical examples of people OFFERING it up to God. And these are people that God really, REALLY loved a lot. Besides, whether you can lose it or it can be taken from you is entirely different than whether you can lay it down. Jesus said, "No man takes my life, I lay it down willingly." (John 10:17) Clearly, Jesus was aiming at a TOTAL sacrifice and TOTAL trust in the Father, not just His earthly body. He took on ALL the sins of all men for all time. He had to know that He couldn't go in front of the Father like that! For someone who had been in the Father's presence for eternity, even an instant of separation had to be excruciating beyond anything we can imagine! I believe that the sacrifice Jesus made in the spiritual realms was FAR more awe-inspiring than even what His physical body endured.

You HAVE to believe that God might actually take you up on it and send you to hell. You have to believe that He might actually take all your gifts away and give them to someone else. And you have to be OK with that because you trust God with all your heart and believe that He knows best. I don't think people are preaching the MAXIMUM application of the love for each other that Jesus modeled. I have never heard this from any pulpit or on any tape or CD or conference anywhere. Whatever I have learned about this kind of love, came from no man.

In His last bit of time on earth with His disciples, Jesus repeated the same message over and over and over in a very short period of time (this isn't even all of them!). It might make a lot of sense for us to listen to it and apply it. He said:

> John 13:34-35 – *"A new command I give you: Love one another. As I have loved you, so you must love one another. By this all men will know that you are my disciples, if you love one another."*

> John 14:12-14 – *"I tell you the truth, anyone who has faith in me will do what I have been doing. He will do even greater things than these, because I am going to the Father. And I will do whatever you ask in my name, so that the Son may bring glory to the Father. You may ask me for anything in my name and I will do it."*

> John 14:15 – *"If you love me, you will obey what I command."*

John 14:21 – *"Whoever has my commands and obeys them, he is the one who loves me. He who loves me will be loved by my Father, and I too will love him and show myself to him."*

John 14:23-24 – *"If anyone loves me, he will obey my teaching. My Father will love him, and we will come to him and make our home with him. He who does not love me will not obey my teaching. These words you hear are not my own; they belong to the Father who sent me."*

John 15:12-13 – *"My command is this: Love each other as I have loved you. Greater love has no one than this, that he lay down his life for his friends. You are my friends if you do what I command."*

John 15:17 – *"This is my command: Love each other."*

Could it be more clear? In real time, this talk to His disciples probably only took a few minutes, but over and over He's pounding this same note! Can't you imagine that if you were there His body language and tone would be one of imploring and urgently requesting them to burn this into their minds and apply it? Don't you think He wanted them to remember this VERY clearly? They were going to need a lot of love to get through the next few days, but it surely has application to us and the hard days that we have ahead as well. We MUST learn to love each other as HE loved us.

I don't think we really understand what He did for us. The "Passion of the Christ" movie is graphic and it moves many people to a better understanding of what He endured physically, but it's just a tiny piece of the true battle that was raging in the spiritual realms and the massive weight that He took on Himself for our sakes. The Son of God laid down His eternal birthright out of His love for us and took on all of the suffering that was due to us. If we are going to be like Him and fully obey Him and LOVE like He did – then maybe we need to be willing to drink from the cup He drank from. Do you think you can?

Well, you can't. Not without a great big cup full of Jesus. The YOU in your cup can't pray that, but the JESUS in you can. He already did. He's really good at it. All you have to do is get the YOU out of the way and watch what happens. People will say that we shouldn't seek after spiritual gifts, we should just love each other. They will refer to I Corinthians 13, the "Love Chapter," to prove that all that flashy Holy Spirit stuff is meaningless and we just need love. Or they will even use this chapter to say that when the Bible was completed, that which was perfect has come, so that which was in part (tongues and prophecy) was done away. But if that were the case, we would have put away childish things and all you have to do is look around to see that we haven't. We clearly do not "know fully" and this system that we have built clearly isn't seeing "face to face," so I don't think the Bible being completed is what Paul was talking about. I think He means that when the fullness of God's love is made real in you, THEN you see face to face.

Besides, you can't just ignore that this beautiful chapter is bracketed immediately on BOTH sides by a command to desire more and greater Gifts (charisma).

> I Corinthians 12:27-31 – *27 Now you are the body of Christ, and each one of you is a part of it. 28 And in the church God has appointed first of all apostles, second prophets, third teachers, then workers of miracles, also those having gifts of healing, those able to help others,*

those with gifts of administration, and those speaking in different kinds of tongues. 29 Are all apostles? Are all prophets? Are all teachers? Do all work miracles? 30 Do all have gifts of healing? Do all speak in tongues? Do all interpret? 31 <u>But eagerly desire the greater gifts</u>. And now I will show you the most excellent way.

1 Corinthians 13 – *1 If I speak in the tongues of men and of angels, but have not love, I am only a resounding gong or a clanging cymbal. 2 If I have the gift of prophecy and can fathom all mysteries and all knowledge, and if I have a faith that can move mountains, but have not love, I am nothing. 3 If I give all I possess to the poor and surrender my body to the flames, but have not love, I gain nothing. 4 Love is patient, love is kind. It does not envy, it does not boast, it is not proud. 5 It is not rude, it is not self-seeking, it is not easily angered, it keeps no record of wrongs. 6 Love does not delight in evil but rejoices with the truth. 7 It always protects, always trusts, always hopes, always perseveres. 8 Love never fails. But where there are prophecies, they will cease; where there are tongues, they will be stilled; where there is knowledge, it will pass away. 9 For we know in part and we prophesy in part, 10 but when perfection comes, the imperfect disappears. 11 When I was a child, I talked like a child, I thought like a child, I reasoned like a child. When I became a man, I put childish ways behind me. 12 Now we see but a poor reflection as in a mirror; then we shall see face to face. Now I know in part; then I shall know fully, even as I am fully known. 13 And now these three remain: faith, hope and love. But the greatest of these is love.*

I Corinthians 14:1-5 – *1 Follow the way of love and* <u>*eagerly desire spiritual gifts, especially the gift of*</u> <u>*prophecy.*</u> *2 For anyone who speaks in a tongue does not speak to men but to God. Indeed, no one understands him; he utters mysteries with his spirit. 3 But everyone who prophesies speaks to men for their strengthening, encouragement and comfort. 4 He who speaks in a tongue edifies himself, but he who prophesies edifies the church. 5 I would like every one of you to speak in tongues, but I would rather have you prophesy. He who prophesies is greater than one who speaks in tongues, unless he interprets, so that the church may be edified.*

The instruction in I Corin. 14:1-5 couldn't be more clear. Follow the way of love **AND** eagerly desire spiritual gifts! ESPECIALLY prophecy! But didn't Paul just say prophecy was going to cease and tongues were like a clanging symbol? No, he didn't say that. He said it would EVENTUALLY cease when the perfect had come – which it hasn't or else we'd all be walking in pure LOVE. (Oh, c'mon! It just hasn't! Stop holding on so tight to a doctrine of Man! Scripture interprets Scripture and you can't find anywhere else that it says the Gifts of the Spirit were just for that time and don't apply to us now! I love you, but let it go!) What he said was that if the Gifts are not operated with, by and through LOVE, they are useless.

Since Paul lectures about tongues and prophecy on either side of this chapter and brackets this chapter with exhortations to seek more and better Gifts (charisma), I just don't see how this argument can be used against what I'm proposing here. If you see something I don't, feel free to email us anytime – fotm@fellowshipofthemartyrs.com .

Anyway, I think we see the fulfillment of Chapter 13 when the Body of Christ starts laying down EVERYTHING for each other. If I have a great gift of prophecy, if I have knowledge, if I have wisdom, if I have tongues, if I have a calling and an anointing and I'm willing to lay it all down and pour it out onto a brother or sister, even unto my own salvation – then I think we're getting about as close to the fulfillment of this chapter as we can get in this life. People that can pray that kind of stuff and really mean it are not going to be self-serving, rude, boasting, proud, delight in evil or keep a record of wrongs. They would most likely protect, trust, hope, persevere and never, ever fail. I believe that's where we're headed. I hope you can join us. God has prepared a lot of people like that for a time such as this.

If you're buying any of this, let's pray.

Father God, You alone are worthy. We see more and more every day what You did for us by sacrificing Your Son for us and what Jesus did by coming as the Christ and laying everything down for us. Give us an enlarged understanding of the sacrifice made on our behalf and renew a right spirit within us. Make us the kind of people that will lay anything down at any moment to further Your Kingdom. Not for our glory, but for Yours. This is a hard saying, Lord. Few can walk it. Teach us how to pray the really big prayers. Help us to be so full of Jesus that He can pray through us. Anything in us that gets in the way, please get it out. Whatever it takes. Just make us like Jesus in the biggest possible way. Teach us to love as You love us. Try us and refine us by sending people that are really hard to love. Whatever it takes. In the mighty name of Jesus Christ, Amen

FEAR OF THE LORD AXIOMS

You may feel like just skipping to the Spiritual Gifts stuff, but I'm telling you, you BETTER get this straight in your head. You BETTER get more Fear of the Lord as quickly as possible before you move on through this!! Please hear me, go read the warning label again. Fear of the Lord is the BEGINNING of Wisdom. Without it you could really mess up whatever He gives you or ask with the wrong heart and get something ugly. Humor me, I learned this the hard way.

IF we sin, **THEN** we must not have enough Fear of the Lord. (The Father AND the Son.)

IF we don't have enough fear of the Lord, **THEN** it must be because we don't see Him clearly.

IF we don't see Him clearly, **THEN** it must be because we have been deceived about who He really is.

IF we have been deceived, **THEN** we are worshiping another Jesus.

IF we are worshiping another Jesus, **THEN** we are not saved.

IF we are not saved, **THEN** we will go to hell.

IF we believe many in the church, **THEN** we accept Jesus into our hearts as our personal Savior.

IF Jesus is our Savior from that moment on, **THEN** there is no need for any further action on our part.

IF the act of accepting Him as Savior is sufficient, **THEN** we can do whatever we want after that.

IF it is a one-time thing and a completed work, **THEN** there is no further need for obedience to Him.

IF we say "Lord, Lord" but mean Savior, **THEN** He may not acknowledge us before God.

IF we believe the Bible, **THEN** we accept Jesus as our Lord and Master.

IF Jesus is our Lord, **THEN** we are entirely at His mercy and direction thereafter.

IF we accept Jesus as our Lord, **THEN** He will acknowledge us before the Father.

IF we accept Jesus as Lord, **THEN** He will fight our battles and His nature in us will keep us from sin.

IF we fully accept Jesus as Lord, **THEN** He can direct ALL our paths.

IF we declare Him to be Savior, **THEN** we place Him in a position of one-time needfulness.

IF we declare Him as Savior, **THEN** we leave open the position and title of Lord.

IF Jesus is not Lord, **THEN** we won't look to Him for daily direction.

IF we're not looking to Him for daily direction, **THEN** we will look elsewhere.

IF the position and title of Lord is vacant, **THEN** some Man will try to become that over us.

IF the position and title of Lord is vacant, **THEN** the religious establishment leadership benefits most.

IF the religious establishment preaches Savior, **THEN** it may be because they want to be Lord.

IF we accept any Man as our Lord, **THEN** we are at their whim.

IF we are at the whim of Man, **THEN** we will not have peace and joy and victory.

IF we do not have peace and joy and victory, **THEN** we are under the control of the enemy.

IF we're under the control of the enemy, **THEN** we're on the wrong team – even if we fed poor people.

IF we're on the wrong team, **THEN** Jesus will not acknowledge us before the Father.

IF we had a little fear of the Lord, **THEN** we would see that He is Sovereign and there is no other.

IF we had more fear of the Lord, **THEN** we would hate the "world" and everything in it and seek Him only.

IF we had lots of fear of the Lord, **THEN** we would weep and mourn and groan for days for the massive blackness of our hearts (individually and collectively) and the distance between us and Him.

IF we had fear of the Lord, **THEN** we would have the beginning of wisdom.

IF we had the beginning of wisdom, **THEN** we wouldn't be tossed by every wind of doctrine.

IF we had the beginning of wisdom, **THEN** we would pray that He would give us more fear of the Lord.

IF He gives us more fear of the Lord, **THEN** it's really, really going to hurt.

IF we love Him and want truth above all, **THEN** we'll keep asking anyway.

SINGLE-USE SAVIOR OR KING, COMMANDER, LORD?

John 8:24 - *"I told you that you would die in your sins; if you do not believe that **I am the one I claim to be**, you will indeed **die** in your sins."*

2 Timothy 4:3-4 – *For the time will come when men will not put up with sound doctrine. Instead, to suit their own desires, they will gather around them a great number of teachers to say what their itching ears want to hear. They will turn their ears away from the truth and turn aside to myths.*

Luke 9:23-24 – *Then he said to them all, "If anyone would come after me, he **must deny himself** and **take up his cross daily** and **follow me**. For whoever wants to save his life will lose it, but whoever loses his life for me will save it."*

Romans 6:6 – *For we know that our old self was crucified with him so that the body of sin might be done away with, that we should **no longer** be slaves to sin.*

Luke 14:33 – *In the same way, any of you who does not **give up everything** he has **cannot** be my disciple.*

Ephesians 4:22-24 – *You were taught, with regard to your former way of life, **to put off your old self**, which is being corrupted by its deceitful desires; to **be made new** in the attitude of your minds; and to **put on the new self**, created to **be like God in true righteousness and holiness**.*

Romans 10:9 – *If you confess with your mouth, "Jesus is **LORD**," **and believe** in your heart that God raised him from the dead, you will be saved."*

2 Corin. 4:5 – *We do not preach ourselves, but Jesus Christ as **LORD**."*

I Corin. 8:5-6 – *Even if there are so-called gods, whether in heaven or on earth (as indeed there are many "gods" and many "lords"), yet for us there is but **one God**, the Father, from whom all things came and for whom we live; and there is but **one Lord**, Jesus Christ, through whom all things came and through whom we live.*

Romans 10:13 – *And everyone who calls upon the name of the **LORD** will be saved.*

Philippians 2:10-11 – *Therefore God exalted him to the highest place and gave him the name that is above every name, that at the name of Jesus **every** knee should bow, in heaven and on earth and under the earth, and **every** tongue confess that Jesus Christ is **LORD**, to the glory of God the Father.*

Revelation 17:14 – *They will make war against the Lamb, but the Lamb will overcome them because he is the **LORD** of lords and **King** of kings – and with him will be his called, chosen and faithful followers.*

John 20:28 – *Thomas said to him, "My **LORD** and my **God**!"*

Revelation 19:11-16 – *I saw heaven standing open and there before me was a white horse, whose rider is called Faithful and True. With justice he judges and makes war. His eyes are like blazing fire, and on his head are many crowns. He has a name written on him that no one knows but he himself. He is dressed in a robe dipped in blood, and his name is the Word of God. The armies of heaven were following him, riding on white horses and dressed in fine linen, white and clean. Out of his mouth comes a sharp sword with which to strike down the nations. "He will rule them with an iron scepter." He treads the winepress of the fury of the wrath of God Almighty. On his robe and on his thigh he has this name written: **KING OF KINGS AND LORD OF LORDS.***

There is no need to have "Fear of a Savior". Why fear a lifeguard at the beach? But the Bible specifically says that "Fear of the LORD is the beginning of wisdom." Please pray that He would be LORD of your life in every way - King, Commander, Ruler, LORD. He's a Monarch. You bow before a Monarch. You come humbly. Don't toy with Him. He's really big.

Number of Usages of the Titles of Jesus in Scripture

Lord – 618	Christ – 543	Son of Man – 84
Teacher – 42	Son of God – 37	King – 35
Lamb – 32	**Savior – 15**	Prophet – 15
Master – 11		

*(**Source:** What the Bible says about a Saving Faith, Koerselman – www.BereanPublishers.com – book online free)*

FAITH LIKE A TEENAGER

We have three different, identical accounts of Jesus' clear statement that you WILL NOT enter into the kingdom of God unless you receive it like a little child.

> Matt. 18:3 *And said, Verily I say unto you, Except ye be converted, and become as little children, ye shall not enter into the kingdom of heaven.*

> Mark 10:15 *Verily I say unto you, Whosoever shall not receive the kingdom of God as a little child, he shall not enter therein.*

> Luke 18:17 *Verily I say unto you, Whosoever shall not receive the kingdom of God as a little child shall in no wise enter therein.*

IF the Word of God is true and right, THEN this is a pretty darn critical point and you might want to really, really be sure that you are getting this right!

So, how are you doing on this point? Do you have faith like a child? Perhaps a parable will help.

FaithLikeAChild sits in the back of the minivan and looks out the window and goes, "Whee!" FaithLikeAChild doesn't know how the engine works or where gasoline comes from and does not worry about whether the minivan has side air bags. FaithLikeAChild just knows that Dad is driving and we're going to Grandma's house and we're stopping at McDonald's on the way! FaithLikeAChild doesn't know how to navigate the route and doesn't care. FaithLikeAChild would never even consider trying to drive – it never even occurred to FaithLikeAChild that Dad wasn't fully capable of getting the job done all by himself. FaithLikeAChild just peacefully dozes off and enjoys the ride, even if it's bumpy. Nothing to worry about, because Dad knows what He's doing. FaithLikeAChild chatters with Dad and hangs on his every word because FaithLikeAChild adores Dad. Dad is his provider, rescuer, leader and generally his real life superhero. Regardless of any physical or logical evidence to the contrary, FaithLikeAChild is just sure that his Dad can beat up your Dad.

If you want to see another picture of FaithLikeAChild, try this:

> Mark 4: 37-40 – A*nd a furious storm of wind arose, and the waves kept beating into the boat, so that it was already becoming filled. But He [Jesus] was in the stern of the boat, asleep on the cushion; and they awoke Him and said to Him, Master, do You not care that we are perishing? And He arose and rebuked the wind and said to the sea, Hush now! Be still! And the wind ceased and there was immediately a great calm. He said to them, Why are you so timid and fearful? How is it that you have no faith?*

FaithLikeAChild was the other name of that kid with a slingshot that said this to a monster named Goliath:

1 Sam. 17:26, 37, 46, 48

Who is this uncircumcised Philistine that he should defy the armies of the living God. The Lord who delivered me from the paw of the lion and the paw of the bear will deliver me from the hand of this Philistine. "This day the Lord will hand you over to me and I'll strike you down and cut off your head." Then as the Philistine moved closer to attack him, David ran quickly to the battle line to meet him.

And lots like him – Abraham, Noah, Moses, Joseph, Daniel, Gideon, Samson, Peter, Stephen and many more throughout history. FaithLikeAChild speaks boldly and fearlessly and RUNS QUICKLY to the battle line to meet the enemy. FaithLikeAChild doesn't worry about fancy armor or battle strategy, FaithLikeAChild knows that God can use anything and so he goes against the giants in the strength that he has - even a slingshot and five stones. FaithLikeAChild is supremely offensive to others because he is the most like Jesus. People think he is arrogant, foolish, senseless, suicidal, childish, short-sighted, capricious, unpredictable and generally impossible to deal with. As soon as Goliath saw David, he despised him (I Sam. 17:42). David's brothers burned with anger towards him (I Sam 17:28). Saul hated him (I Sam 18:8-11 and elsewhere). There is no end of trouble when you start accepting the Kingdom of God like a little child! And no end to the reward.

Though sadly, FaithLikeATeenager is far more common. FaithLikeATeenager doesn't want to sit in the back of the minivan, he just got his license and he wants to drive himself.

FaithLikeATeenager pesters Dad to get into the passenger seat. FaithLikeATeenager doesn't want to go to McDonald's because it isn't healthy and he can't believe that Dad is unaware of the ecological and economic and human justice damage that a fascist global conglomerate like that is doing to the world. Poor old Dad is just not as well-informed as FaithLikeATeenager. In fact, sometimes FaithLikeATeenager wonders how Dad ever got along without him. FaithLikeATeenager doesn't particularly want to go to Grandma's house, but is just sure that he knows a quicker way to get there. FaithLikeATeenager doesn't doze off and enjoy the ride. FaithLikeATeenager turns the music up really loud, makes a call on his cell phone, drinks his organic, Fair Trade, wheat germ smoothie, drives too fast and tries hard to ignore Dad as much as possible. FaithLikeATeenager is just sure that he has all the answers and his way is best. In fact, he would really like it if Dad would just shut up and leave him alone. He is his own superhero.

FaithLikeAChild knows that he is completely safe because Dad is in control. FaithLikeATeenager thinks he is indestructible because he is really smart and cool. Which one do you think Dad would rather hang out with?

Why does it seem like God is moving in greater ways in Africa and India and China? Maybe because there are more people there named FaithLikeAChild. Why do we have tens of thousands of denominations in America and endless conferences and programs and books and superstar leaders? Maybe because we are the capital of FaithLikeATeenager. In fact, we're the main producer and exporter worldwide. We're building fatter and fatter pipelines so we can pump all of our own special flavors of it into every country on the planet.

Are there any seminaries in America that have a "FaithLikeAChild" degree? Who were the experts in FaithLikeATeenager in Jesus' time? The Pharisees and the Sadducees. The religious leaders are always the ones that think they're all grown up and that they know best. Go read Matthew 23 and see how Jesus felt about them. He's pretty clear about how He feels about FaithLikeATeenager. You better hope you're not one of them.

How about this?

> Matthew 7:21-23 – *"Not everyone who says to me, 'Lord, Lord,' will enter the kingdom of heaven, but only he who does the will of my Father who is in heaven. Many will say to me on that day, 'Lord, Lord, did we not prophesy in your name, and in your name drive out demons and perform many miracles?' Then I will tell them plainly, 'I never knew you. Away from me, you evildoers!'*

If this is really true, then we might want to be listening to Dad more and obeying Him and not going our own way. Many will think that they are just fine – until they are told to their face that their new name is "FaithLikeATeenager" and that it has all been in vain.

God is raising up the true warriors. Those who will not question or doubt. Those who will go, no matter who says they are nuts. God is raising up an army of children with nothing holding them down. Children who will fearlessly wade into the battle with a slingshot (and an army of angels). They will kill the Goliaths (and the status quo) without mercy or pity. They will obey fully because the Lamb is their head. They will not argue theology or doctrine or curriculum or programs. They will just listen to the voice of God and obey. And they will bring a flame-thrower to all the structures and systems of FaithLikeATeenager. Nothing will be able to stand before them – because God is on their side.

Just in case you're sitting on the fence about this when they come, consider this:

> Matthew 18:3-6 – *And he said: "I tell you the truth, unless you change and become like little children, you will never enter the kingdom of heaven. Therefore, whoever humbles himself like this child is the greatest in the kingdom of heaven. "And whoever welcomes a little child like this in my name welcomes me. But if anyone causes one of these little ones who believe in me to sin, it would be better for him to have a large millstone hung around his neck and to be drowned in the depths of the sea.*

Or maybe this one:

> Luke 9:46-48 – *An argument started among the disciples as to which of them would be the greatest. Jesus, knowing their thoughts, took a little child and had him stand beside him. Then he said to them, "Whoever welcomes this little child in my name welcomes me; and whoever welcomes me welcomes the one who sent me. For he who is least among you all—he is the greatest."*

Just stop for a minute and look around and see if you or your congregation or denomination are arguing with anybody else about who is the greatest. See if you are letting God direct your paths or you are leaning on your own understanding. Proverbs 3:5-6 is pretty clear.

> Proverbs 3:5-6 – *Trust in the LORD with all thine heart; and lean not unto thine own understanding. In all thy ways acknowledge him, and he shall direct thy paths.*

All means <u>ALL</u>. None of your own understanding is acceptable. <u>None</u> of you directing your own paths is OK. Doing so means that you are not trusting the Lord your God with ALL your heart. And it means that your new name is FaithLikeATeenager and God is going to write it on your forehead. The first being in history to earn that name was Lucifer. If God writes that on your forehead – then, congratulations, you just got the mark of the beast.

If that's your name, even a little bit, then you might want to say you're sorry and beg the Lord to scrub it off your forehead and ask Him daily to kill anything in you that is more than about six years old – give or take.

THE BEATITUDES AND YOUR CUP – MATTHEW 5:3-12

The Lord showed me very clearly how Matthew 5 intersects with the understandings about "cups" and cup management. I hope that I can express this as clearly as He showed it to me. (See graphic at bottom of this writing.)

You need to understand that the Beatitudes, as with nearly all of the Word of God have multiple applications on various levels. Like spirals – repeating parallel cycles but different applications. Seen that way, the largest possible application is to the spiritual/eternal – not the natural/temporary.

3 *"Blessed are the poor in spirit, for theirs is the kingdom of heaven.*

First you need to note that it doesn't say "Spirit," it says "spirit". He's not at all saying that you are blessed if you are poor in HIS Spirit! You are blessed if there is hardly any YOU in your cup so that HE can fill all the available space! You are blessed when you are poured out and there is hardly any of you left at all. Yours is the kingdom of heaven when there is practically none of You to get in His way. He can use you mightily when you have given Him all of your false riches (knowledge, experience, personality, charisma, degrees, dreams, etc.) and are left with only the bare minimum (faith like a child). Then He can pour in the true riches of HIS Spirit. The less of YOU there is, the more room there will be for JESUS to fill.

4 *Blessed are those who mourn, for they will be comforted.*

What are they mourning about? The death of a loved one? That hardly seems to fit here. This is all about eternal and spiritual things, why mourn about the death of a jar of clay? I think this applies to those who are mourning for souls, mourning for the sad state of things and desperate state of the mess we've made of our own hearts, our families, our churches, our cities, our world. I think this is a reference to those in Ezekiel 9 that are the ONLY ones spared from the wrath of God poured out on the lukewarm and asleep. You can see that the first fruits in Revelation 7, the 144,000, are those who are comforted. I suspect they are the ones mourning the most. If you truly see through the eyes of Jesus (because you have hardly any of You left and a big cup of Jesus), then you will almost surely mourn for how much God is grieved and hurt by what we're doing (or not doing). It's very dark out there and it's our fault.

5 *Blessed are the meek, for they will inherit the earth.*

Humility is an unavoidable by-product of having practically none of You left and a big cup of Jesus. The more we realize the distance between us and God and how truly big and merciful and holy and just and faithful He is, the more we <u>must</u> be meek. Those who recognize this and are thrilled to just have the crumbs under the table or stay outside and serve quietly will be ones sitting at the head of the table. Said in reverse, "Cursed are those who are full of pride and self, for they will be cast into outer darkness." Meekness/humility is a clear, internal understanding that pride is the enemy and when it rises up in us it is antichrist. Meekness begs for God to kill the YOU in your cup.

6 Blessed are those who hunger and thirst for righteousness, for they will be filled.

Those who are desperate to keep Sin out of their cup are those who will have maximum capacity to hold more Jesus. You will be filled to the degree that you are hungry and thirsty to be filled and seek out how best to pour it back out. The more you go to the River to drink your fill, the less room there will be for unrighteousness to fit inside. If you understand that Jesus is in your cup and that He doesn't like to be in there with the nasty, icky stuff, you would seek to keep it cleansed and sanctified at every moment. You cannot displace Sin effectively by a force of will, you need to be so full of Jesus that nothing else can fit!

7 Blessed are the merciful, for they will be shown mercy.

This is the action step that proves that your cup is full of Jesus. You must see that others may not have as big a cup or may have embedded Sin that needs to come out and you must lovingly urge them forward as someone that has been there and not self-righteously as someone who knows it all. You must even be willing to stand in the gap for them and take on their burdens if necessary so as to free them. Oppressions that keep them from fully tasting the goodness of God need to be broken or you need to help bear their burden. The more you pour yourself out onto those in need – the more you sacrificially give of all that you have, even if you don't get it back – the more God will expand your cup and pour out on you. The more He will grant you mercy when you mess things up and act prideful and rebellious.

8 *Blessed are the pure in heart, for they will see God.*

Those who meet the qualifications above; who have been poured out, who weep for the sad state of things, who have crucified pride, who beg for more Jesus, who regularly pour themselves out and get bigger cups – THOSE are the people who will see God. Others may have dreams and visions or angelic visitations, but THESE are the people who really see God for who He is and have true relationship. These are the ones that He calls, "Friends."

9 *Blessed are the peacemakers, for they will be called the sons of God.*

Above all, these will be like Jesus, because they have the biggest cup of Jesus. And Jesus was a peacemaker with a sword. Peace is not always instant. Sometimes you have to speak the truth in love and know that in the big picture peace will eventually be the result. When Jesus overturned the tables in the Temple it was so that there would be peace there – but it might require 2000+ years for it to materialize. We must always seek His peace – and His ways are not our ways. Sometimes peace doesn't mean being polite and pretending we all agree. Said differently, we are to be at peace with the spirit of our brother, but war against his evil deeds and his rulers. (Psalm 141:5-6)

10 *Blessed are those who are persecuted because of righteousness, for theirs is the kingdom of heaven.*

This is an unavoidable by-product of having a big cup of Jesus and being a peacemaker. See John 15 and I John – and the whole history of the Church, for that matter. The more you are filled with Jesus, the more you will be persecuted. The spirits of this world fear Him intensely and will do everything they can directly or through other people to kill, smother or marginalize the Light in you. If you have a little candle, a couple of bugs might come to see what's going on. If you are the halogen array on top of a football stadium, every bug for MILES is going to come and try to smother you. The bigger your cup, the more Jesus in you, the more the warfare will increase. Guaranteed.

11 *Blessed are you when people insult you, persecute you and falsely say all kinds of evil against you because of me.*

Jesus knows what He went through and how hard it was. He sympathizes and He protects those who endure such things. And you get maximum treasure in heaven for enduring the hardest things for His name! You will be more and more blessed by God the more you are insulted, reviled, assaulted, persecuted, libeled, beaten, burned, boiled, whipped, imprisoned, starved or killed. There is no indication that you will be blessed because you were wealthy.

12 *Rejoice and be glad, because great is your reward in heaven, for in the same way they persecuted the prophets who were before you.*

The Apostle Paul had a great big cup of Jesus and saw a constant stream of miracles around him. He had a LOT of treasure in heaven. To some degree you have to also see that persecution comes so as to further refine us and beat out of us the really deeply entrenched yellow stuff – the You in your cup that really, really doesn't want to budge! Any pride or self-reliance has to be laid down when you have no strength and no one to lean on but God. Through fiery trials He teaches us to be totally and utterly dependent on Him.

When you suffer for the Name of Jesus, you join a great long list of mighty men and women of God who have gone before you. Whether you are physically killed or not, when you ask God to kill all of You that stands in His way, you become a martyr. When He pours You out so that He can pour Himself in, you are truly dead and it's Christ in you that lives. The more you hold back, the less dead you are and the less He can fill you. Rejoice in affliction!! There is no other way to get some of the really stubborn You out! Every time you endure persecution in faith, another ugly chunk of You dies and He can fill the gap with His grace and mercy and peace and gifts of the Spirit. The "Fellowship of the Martyrs" is just the spiritual assembly of those who have died to self and it's Christ in them that lives. Jesus Himself said that sooner or later, people like that will probably also die physically for their faith, but who cares? We're already dead! I pray that God would kill anything in you that is in the way of Him fulfilling His best plans for you.

Which "Cup" do you think the Beatitudes are about?

**I'm sure thinking that
it's THIS ONE! ^ ^ ^**

ALMOST THERE

OK, I know this is taking awhile, but you need to be sure that you got all that. The Cups are real and you need to get cleaned out. You need to pray to get all the SIN out and then keep it out by staying full of Jesus every moment. You need to ask Him to kill all the YOU that might be in His way. You need to ask Him to help you hear His voice REALLY clearly so that He can direct all your paths. We tried to get some more Fear of the Lord in you and make sure you're taking this seriously and motivated by LOVE for Him and for those in need around you. If you're motivated by a desire to have a flashy ministry or to be cool or make money, you're going to be in BIG trouble. (Acts 8:9-24) He wants you broken and contrite and if you're not already, He's going to do it to you. If you sass Him and are rebellious, it's just going to hurt a lot more.

If you say that you're going to give Him ALL and you mean SOME, you may want to go read Acts 5:1-11 again. If you move on from here, the walk is just going to get harder and harder. I'm warning you. You better mean it. This is real.

You ready?

OK, then.

SPIRITUAL GIFT DIALS

We don't have enough Fear of the Lord or we would have a better sense of how intensely complicated this is! We always seek to simplify and compartmentalize God so that we can get our head around Him.

People seem to think the Gifts of the Spirit are on/off switches that you either have or you don't. People actually preach that you may only have one or two gifts, but nobody has ALL of them. And whatever the Holy Spirit gives you, that's what you get and you should be content with it. But I think that's just not scriptural on a whole number of levels.

First, they're not on/off switches, they're <u>dials</u>. There's no other way to explain how someone could have an anointing to heal a headache, but another can regrow a limb or raise the dead. Some have a prophecy gift that just comes as a "deja vu" sort of vague sense of familiarity when something happens and some others see dreams and visions of the future all the time. Some have just enough Gift of Faith to endure a couple weeks without a paycheck and some can endure shipwrecks and torture and jail and total dependence on God for everything. It has to be a spectrum, not a fixed quantity. **I Corinthians 11:11 says that the "Holy Spirit gives them to each one, just as He determines."** That may mean that He gives the Gift itself to those He determines, but it also surely means that He gives it in the <u>quantity</u> that He determines. Sometimes a person gets "dialed up" just long enough for a crisis situation or an immediate need for healing or evangelism or whatever and then may never see that gift again like that. The Holy Spirit's management of each of our Gift's Inventory is a lot more fluid and complicated than we give Him credit for. (I hope that the result of this chapter, too, is more Fear of the Lord.)

Second, Paul specifically instructs us to desire spiritual gifts, especially the big ones that have the biggest impact. He says:

> 1 Corinthians 12:31 – *But covet earnestly the best* (kreitton) *gifts* (charisma):

Remember, Paul is talking to people (the Church in Corinth) that already have SOME spiritual gifts. He encourages them at least twice in this letter to seek more and bigger weapons, especially prophecy.

Best – kreitton {krite'-tohn} – (Strong's 2909)
1) more useful, more serviceable, more advantageous
2) more excellent

Translated as "better" 11 times and only once as "best". Better implies degrees of usefulness. A plurality of possible usefulnesses from among which you should seek the highest possible choice in any given situation.

Gifts – charisma {khar'-is-mah} – (Strong's 5486)

> 1) a favour with which one receives without any merit of his own
> 2) the gift of divine grace
> 3) the gift of faith, knowledge, holiness, virtue
> 4) the economy of divine grace, by which the pardon of sin and eternal salvation is appointed to sinners in consideration of the merits of Christ laid hold of by faith
> 5) grace or gifts denoting extraordinary powers, distinguishing certain Christians and enabling them to serve the church of Christ, the reception of which is due to the power of divine grace operating on their souls by the Holy Spirit

If the Father is willing to give us gifts, we should seek them and be good stewards of them. Jesus doesn't say to wait for the Lord to do everything and never ask. Jesus is clear that we should petition the Father in the name of Jesus for ANYTHING. He tells two different parables about pestering someone until they give in! (Luke 11:5-10 & Luke 18:1-8)

> Luke 11:5-10 – *Then he said to them, "Suppose one of you has a friend, and he goes to him at midnight and says, 'Friend, lend me three loaves of bread, because a friend of mine on a journey has come to me, and I have nothing to set before him.' Then the one inside answers, 'Don't bother me. The door is already locked, and my children are with me in bed. I can't get up and give you anything.' I tell you, though he will not get up and give him the bread because he is his friend, yet because of the man's boldness he will get up and give him as much as he needs. So I say to you: Ask and it will be given to you; seek and you will find;*

knock and the door will be opened to you. For everyone that asks receives; he who seeks finds; and to him who knocks, the door will be opened."

Can it be any more clear that if you don't <u>have</u>, it's because you don't <u>ask</u>? If you have a sincere heart and you just want more of the Holy Spirit, He's not going to give you a demon! He can't. He's a good Dad. You CANNOT get a demon in you by asking God for Spiritual Gifts with a pure heart. Need proof?

Luke 11:11-13 - *"Which of you fathers, if you son asks for a fish, will give him a snake instead? Or if he asks for an egg, will give him a scorpion? If you then, though you are evil, know how to give good gifts to your children, how much more will your Father in heaven give the Holy Spirit to those who ask him!"*

Snakes and scorpions are metaphors for demons. (Look it up, I don't have time to go over all that right now.)

Now, is it possible that you could have someone lay hands on you and get something that isn't from God? Yes. I've seen it happen. If you weren't satan, wouldn't you want undercover agents inside the churches handing out fake gifts? Or worse, Trojan horses that would cause nothing but trouble in somebody, but they think it's from God?

I've met people that had traveling evangelists or leaders of various sorts of ministries lay hands on them to receive tongues and what they got was definitely NOT of God. I heard a guy pray once and I didn't get an interpretation but the Lord instantly put a very clear picture in my mind of the elves in J.R.R. Tolkien's "Lord of the Rings." It was a really beautiful, flowing language and it definitely had power because all the hair on my arm stood up! But it was ELF – and in case anybody asks you, God doesn't give people ELF! This brother had had years and years of trouble with his tongue and being constantly misunderstood and his ministry could never get going because he seemed to always be sticking his foot in his mouth. But it didn't affect everybody and was so strange that I was sure it had to be supernatural. As it happened, he had received this Gift from someone he didn't really know and his walk with God and relationships with people around him had been devastatingly hard ever since. It wasn't just that it had control over his prayers. Since he had given legal ground over his tongue to a demonic force, it could mangle everything he said all the time. He made perfect sense to me most of the time, but some kind of supernatural garbler or "filter" would just tweak what he said so that certain people would always hear it the wrong way! It was really weird.

Whenever I'm doing a full "tune-up" with someone, I always want to listen to whatever prayer language they have (if they realize they have one). If we had more people with the gift of interpretation of tongues, we would know about all the people that speak in church and are actually cursing the pastor or the people! (I've heard of that, even though I haven't experienced that one myself.) Demons know all the languages that ever were, so it's nothing for one of them to speak through someone that has allowed them legal ground. Can you receive a false gift of tongues? Yes.

Ok, so did I just contradict myself? Not exactly. If your heart is pure and you ask the Father directly in the name of Jesus, He'll give you the good stuff. If you ask someone to lay hands on you to receive it, you still make sure YOU are asking the

Father for it and not just letting them push it at you. You need to also "armor up" all the time.

Paul cautions Timothy to: (KJV)

> I Tim. 5:22 – *Lay hands suddenly on no man, neither be partaker of other men's sins: keep thyself pure.*

The argument that I have always heard is that that is a reference to the ordination of deacons or elders, but it's pretty obvious that there were times when Timothy had people lay hands on him (or vice versa) for a purpose other than that. Paul desired to go to the Roman's so that he could impart to them spiritual gifts (by the laying on of his hands). So Paul is surely talking about something broader here than just the ordination of elders. That interpretation of this verse is almost exclusively held by the denominations that don't lay hands on people for any other reason. Again, we have de-spiritualized so much of this by our naturalistic explanations. Let's look at the Young's Literal:

> I Timothy 5:22 – *Be laying hands quickly on no one, nor be having fellowship* (koinoneo) *with sins of others; be keeping thyself pure* (hagnos – pure or clean);

The Wycliffe literal says this:

> I Timothy 5:22 – *Put thou hands to no man, neither at once commune* (koinoneo) *thou with other men's sins [Put thou hands to no man soon, neither commune thou with other men's sins]. Keep thyself chaste* (hagnos – pure or clean).

koinoneo {koy-no-neh'-o} – (Strong's 2841)

1) to come into communion or fellowship with, to become a sharer, be made a partner
2) to enter into fellowship, join one's self to an associate, make one's self a sharer or partner

OK, if the context is broader, we need to understand that it's important that we not lay hands on someone to transfer something we're not supposed to – whether a gift or a commissioning for service. Good advice. Listen to God and do what He tells you. It also means that we need to be very careful about who we allow to lays hands on US. We need to have an assurance from the Lord that it's OK. If you can't hear God, then you're just going to have to go on observation and what you know about the person – but that's not definitive. Best to hear straight from God.

I believe that what Paul is saying is that Timothy should be careful to make sure that he doesn't receive anything bad from someone. To make sure that you are prayerful and careful and armored up so that the sins (or demons) or soul-force or self of a person doesn't pollute your nice clean cup.

You have to understand that Paul did NOT write as one coming from a "naturalistic" standpoint. He was hyper-spiritual and walked it all the time. He had seen Jesus (probably far more than once), had visited heaven and seen things he couldn't repeat, seen thousands healed, raised the dead, fought pagan strongholds, done war with demons of all shapes and sizes, he even inferred to the Corinthians that when he was away he was still among them in the spirit. Do you think that's weird? Everything that the enemy has is a cheap imitation of something God has. But we get the good stuff! They can put a curse on someone's body, we can heal them instantly. They can make a zombie, but we can raise them fully. They can do astral projection and be somewhere else in the spirit, but we can be taken up into heaven or travel supernaturally wherever the Lord takes us. They are spent by their efforts and die young because it's soul-force, but we are energized and victorious because it's Christ in us that lives and reigns!

Ok, follow along. I was just explaining this to a sister the other day who had been raised in a home full of witchcraft. The real stuff, not somebody that just liked crystals and horoscopes. She never understood it before, but the Lord showed her all in a flash that when she was a little girl her mother taught her how to put her hands on someone and transfer spirits to them. They could feel it too, they would know that they had received stuff. And it was BAD stuff that created a soul-tie and gave the kid power and control over that person. This is just elemental stuff if you're into witchcraft. They understand VERY clearly that spirits can be transferred from objects or through people. All kinds of spirits – all bad. (If you really aren't sure I'm telling the truth, then armor up really good with the Blood of Jesus and do a Google search online for "witch + transference".) There's also repeated Biblical commands to keep defiled objects out of your home or you and your home (and the land) will become defiled and bring curses on you.

If you're in a "Spirit-filled" denomination, this shouldn't be weird at all. You understand that we can lay hands on someone and bless them and the Holy Spirit moves through us. Jesus did it all the time. All the apostles and hundreds of millions of Christians since have seen/felt the Holy Spirit flow through them in this way – either as the recipient or the conduit.

The problem is that we don't always armor up in church when someone lays hands on us because we don't think that anything bad could get on us (or in us). We'd never allow it from a stranger at the mall, but we can have a whole huddle of 20 people (some we don't know) praying over us for healing in church. I'm convinced that those "huddles" are a really bad idea. First, the elders and those who have an anointing for the need in question should be the only ones necessary. And second, it exposes a whole bunch of people to potential danger. Until everyone is educated about how to make sure that they are sealed up good and protected from anything that someone might push at them – intentionally or not – it would be better to limit the number of people making spiritual contact like that.

I'm under a standing order from God that whatever congregation I visit, if there is a call for people to go down front for prayer, I'm to go. First, I could use all the prayer I can get, but I'm also there to see what happens. Maybe somebody gets a word from the Lord for me – or maybe I uncover something icky that shouldn't be there. Either way, I go down front FULLY armored up, all the doors shut tight and covered in the Blood of Jesus. I pray that nothing OTHER than exactly what the Lord wants for me to have would be able to get through and anybody that's praying bad stuff that it would bounce.

I'm aware of several times when people came as friends to pray with me and they really had malicious intent. Not witches or satanists, but they still were praying with ulterior motives and hoping that something I was doing would fail or with a gloating spirit at my (momentary and light) misfortunes. They might have been praying for help and healing, but something in them was enjoying seeing me suffering. We can speak curses on people by our gossip or even by our prayers that seek something other than God's will for a person. We can even impart our own soulish nature and create a dangerous soul-tie to a person. Our soul-force is dangerous. We have to be VERY careful to draw a heavy line between using our soulish nature to control things and waiting on the Lord to do it by the power of the Holy Spirit.

(Read the book "The Latent Power of the Soul," by Watchman Nee: www.fellowshipofthemartyrs.com/pdf/latent_power_of_the_soul.pdf)

And that's just assuming that someone isn't a full-on occultist! We have plenty of witches and warlocks and Masons and Klan and others inside our churches. Far more than we realize.

Anybody involved in any of that stuff, to whatever degree, needs to renounce it completely and repent before they can expect to get their cup cleaned out and start hearing God better. If you were hearing Him now, you're hear Him yelling at you to get away from that stuff. Anybody in a leadership role in front of God's sheep that is doing any of that stuff needs to step down immediately and renounce it and prove they mean it. Read all the verses about how God feels about that stuff – www.fellowshipofthemartyrs.com/witchcraft.htm. You better get free from it right away and get full of Jesus. He's not kidding around.

I cannot stress enough how important it is to be fully armored up before giving or receiving anything spiritually. Since you can receive stuff whether you know it or not, it's really critical to be fully armored up all the time. The Blood of Jesus will cover you, so long as you don't invite it in by ignorance or outright rebellion against God.

Pray this (Or something in this general direction. It ain't special or anything):

Lord God, I want You and You only in my life. Break off and crush anything that might be messing with me right now. Any curses or soul-ties or demonic activity has to stop now in the Name of Jesus. Lord, I don't ever want to receive anything from any person (or any object) that isn't purely from Jesus. Please set your wings about me and shield me against anything the enemy is trying to do against me. I stand in faith that the Blood of Jesus is sufficient to protect me against all attacks. Please alert me if someone is trying to harm me in any way. I want to make sure You get the credit and praise and thanks for watching out for me. I know you will and I stand in faith on Your promises of protection and provision. Cover me in the Blood of Jesus now and every day. In the mighty Name of our Lord Jesus Christ, Amen.

OK, back to the point here. There are LOTS of different kinds of gifts, a lot more than people realize, and nearly endless variants and interactivities between them. It's not nearly as cut and dried as people think. I hope that when you get a little glimpse of it this way, you will marvel even more at God's love for you and the complexity of all that the Holy Spirit does inside of you every day, just to manage all this stuff!

2 Peter 1:3 – *According as his divine power* (dunamis) *hath given unto us all things that [pertain] unto life and godliness, through the knowledge of him that hath called us to glory and virtue.*

Hebrews 2:4 – *God also bearing [them] witness, both with signs and wonders, and with divers* (poikilos) *miracles* (dunamis), *and gifts of the Holy Ghost, according to his own will?*

Poikilos is translated here "divers" but defined by Strong's (4164) as:

1) a various colours, variegated
2) of various sorts

It is translated eight times as "divers" and twice as "manifold".

1 Corinthians 12:4 – *Now there are diversities* (diairesis) *of gifts* (charisma), *but the same Spirit.*

1 Corinthians 7:7 – *For I would that all men were even as I myself. But every man hath his proper gift* (charisma) *of God, one after this manner, and another after that.*

1 Corin. 1:7 – *So that ye come behind in no gift ; waiting for the coming of our Lord Jesus Christ:*

So He has given us all things pertaining unto life and godliness, through the knowledge of him that called us to glory and virtue. Did you know you were called to glory and virtue? Isn't that cool?! Yep, so how do we do it? By the dunamis of God. There's no other way.

The Hebrews 2:4 verse also indicates that the miracles and gifts of the Holy Ghost are poikilos – that is, if you seek and find, what you'll probably get is variegated, diverse dunamis – lots of flavors, colors, frequencies, wavelengths! Wow! Not only is the Holy Spirit living inside you, He has to keep track of all this stuff on the fly for your benefit and for the Father's glory.

Romans 12:6-8 (Amplified) – *Having then gifts* (charisma) *differing according to the grace that is given to us, whether prophecy, [let us prophesy] according to the proportion of faith; Or ministry, [let us wait] on [our] ministering: or he that teacheth, on teaching; Or he that exhorteth, on exhortation: he that giveth, [let him do it] with simplicity; he that ruleth, with diligence; he that sheweth mercy, with cheerfulness.*

Here's one of the best verses to confirm and substantiate all of this. Try this on:

2 Corinthians 1:11 – *Ye also helping together by prayer for us, that for the gift* (charisma) *[bestowed] upon us by the means of many persons thanks may be given by many on our behalf.*

Did you get that? The charisma that Paul (and Timothy in this letter) had in them came from having been bestowed on them by MANY persons. This was not just the original Baptism of the Holy Spirit (which Paul got from Ananias in Acts 9:17). And since here Paul uses "we" to indicate both he and Timothy, the clear implication is that both of them had received charisma (Gifts of the Spirit) from many/multiple people. Since Paul also imparted Gifts to Timothy, there must be multiple occasions of this having happened. In fact, Paul was originally ordained and commissioned by the elders in Antioch, not Corinth. But this letter seems to be thanking the Corinthians for having impart Gifts to them!

Remember these?

1 Timothy 4:14 – *Neglect not the gift* (charisma) *that is in thee, which was given thee by prophecy, with the laying on of the hands of the elders.*

2 Timothy 1:6 – *Wherefore I put thee in remembrance that thou stir up the gift* (charisma) *of God, which is in thee by the putting on of my hands.*

Looks like multiple instances of impartation to me. Could it just be a translation problem? Let's try the Darby:

2 Corinthians 1:11 – *ye also labouring together by supplication for us that the gift* (charisma) *towards us, through means of many persons, may be the subject of the thanksgiving of many for us.*

How about Young's Literal?

2 Corinthians 1:11 – *ye working together also for us by your supplication, that the gift* (charisma) *through many persons to us, through many may be thankfully acknowledged for us.*

I wonder how badly the NIV mangles it?

2 Corinthians 2:11 – *as you help us by your prayers. Then many will give thanks on our behalf for the gracious favor granted us in answer to the prayers of many.*

Yep, that's pretty bad. Doesn't even have any sense of it being a charisma at all! Like they're just being polite and sending them with their best wishes. Not really supernatural at all. You need to be really careful with the NIV. It's widely read across the mainline denominations and they're widely spiritually weak. It might not be a coincidence. (A dunamis shortage all around, I think.)

Oh! Just for fun, let's see what "The Message" says:

2 Corinthians 1:11 – *You and your prayers are part of the rescue operation—I don't want you in the dark about that*

either. I can see your faces even now, lifted in praise for God's deliverance of us, a rescue in which your prayers played such a crucial part.

Wow. That practically makes no sense at all! I have no idea what that has to do with gifts of the spirit! Whadaya say we don't quote from that version <u>ever</u> again, OK?

HOW COMPLICATED COULD IT BE?
THERE ARE ONLY A FEW GIFTS
OF THE SPIRIT, RIGHT?

Yeah, you'd think it would be easy wouldn't you? I've seen Spiritual Gift Inventory tests with 20 to 100 questions that help you narrow in on what you're good at. We have those so that we can identify tendencies or behaviors that are ALREADY in place, but not potentialities and future giftings or callings. Basically, we don't really have anointed apostles and prophets and people operating in discernment of spirits in any big enough quantity to just SEE who has what gifts and we (as a whole) don't hear God well enough to just ask Him ourselves. So we have to have psychological inventories. It's really very sad.

Ok, here is the generally agreed upon list:

THE GIFTS AND CALLINGS OF THE HOLY SPIRIT

I Corin. 12:4-14	I Corin. 12:27-30	Rom. 12:6-8	Eph. 4:11
Word of Wisdom	Apostles	Prophecy	Apostles
Word of Knowledge	Prophets	Ministry	Prophets
Faith	Teachers	Teaching	Evangelists
Healings	Miracles	Exhortation	Pastors and
Working of Miracles	Healings	Giving	Teachers*
Prophecy	Helps	Leading	
Discernment of	Administrations	Showing Mercy	
Spirits	Tongues		
Tongues			
Interpretation of			
Tongues			

Note: * Some authorities distinguish between Pastors and Teachers in the list contained in Ephesians. That's how they get a "Five-fold" instead of a "Four-fold" ministry.

There are some others that are a little less clearly stated and some folks disagree with them being added to the list above. They include; hospitality, celibacy, voluntary poverty and exorcism/deliverance (although that is generally classified within the healing gift).

Gifts of the Spirit are not the same as the "fruit of the spirit" (Galatians 5:22). Since the "sign gifts" or manifestation gifts can sometimes be faked or come from evil sources (Matt. 24:24, 7:22-23), the true and better test is of the specific fruit listed here.

Fruit of the Spirit (Galatians. 5:22-23)
Love, Joy, Peace, Longsuffering, Gentleness, Goodness, Faith, Meekness, Temperance.

Please note the things that CANNOT be used to determine spiritual fruit. There are some obvious things <u>missing</u> from this list. Things like; size of ministry, eloquence of speech, new book deal, longevity in office, number of advanced degrees, physical attractiveness or magnetism, material wealth, number of people that agree with them, quantity or size of their miracles, likeability by the "world", etc. If you have been judging someone based on anything OTHER than the Biblical Fruit, you might want to say you're sorry and rethink to whom you've been listening. Jesus said that the more you were like Him, the more you would be hated and persecuted, so someone with lots of the TRUE Fruit is most likely going to be surrounded by a big cloud of controversy and lies. Don't let that automatically scare you off.

Basically, you can't dial up the Fruit of the Spirit. You can impart them to someone – you can share your Peace or Joy or Self-Control, but they have to walk it out before it becomes Fruit. You can pour it (sow it) into them all you want, but it's dead seed until it sprouts and produces a harvest – THEN it's Fruit. Basically, the bigger their "cup" gets, the more they are filled with Jesus, the more these Fruits will manifest because it

is Christ in them that lives and there's not very much of their own selfish, sinful nature to get in the way anymore.

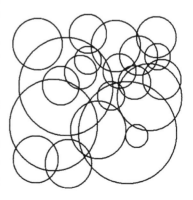

Some of these overlap substantially. You CAN dial up Peace, Joy, Patience because they are things you're "full of" in addition to being

Fruits. Also, you can be full of Mercy and that would drive a bunch of the Fruits (things like Kindness, Generosity, Patience, Gentleness, Faithfulness). Wisdom would drive others (Patience, Modesty, Self-Control, Chastity, Generosity, etc.) Basically, you can take any one of these and replace it with "Jesus" and it retains the same meaning. So more Jesus means more Fruits and more Gifts. Go back and read the chapter about James Dunn (p. 46). Some say there is just ONE Fruit divided in 9 parts. Same difference, the more you look like Jesus, the more this stuff all shows up. But it's important for you to get a sense of how intensely complicated this is. My goal is for you to get so mentally exhausted that you'll stop trying to control or manipulate what God wants and just lay it all at His feet and pour out whatever He tells you, when He tells you. If you try to fiddle with the dials yourself, you'll just make a mess.

Maybe some pictures will help. Imagine that each of these circles is a Spiritual Gift "dial". They interlock and mesh together and overlap in ways we can't even possibly understand. My goal in this book is not to explain exactly how it all works, I don't think any human can. My goal is to motivate people to lovingly share with each as they have a need and to teach AWE and the bigness and complexity of what God is doing in ALL of us.

Can you see that even through the course of a single day, we all are tested and tried and we either pass or fail? We may also meet with people that pray for us, and the Holy Spirit intercedes for us directly with the Father, and maybe we spend time in the Word and receive some spiritual blessing. Throughout the day, this graphic is in constant motion. Like raindrops in a puddle, constantly flowing and rippling and expanding and contracting. Do you really think you can design a Spiritual Gifts inventory that will be accurate a week from now? Only if it is so basic as to be practically useless! (Or you are completely stagnant.)

Do they really overlap like that? Well, I've read about people with a massive gift of healing – people like Smith Wigglesworth, William Branham, James Dunn, Kathryn Kuhlman, Maria Woodworth-Etter, John G. Lake, A. A. Allen and others. (Go look them up online.) They all have their Faith dial up really high – that seems to control most everything. But the ones that seem to keep their head on straight and not start thinking they're Elijah usually also have their Wisdom and Discernment of Spirits dial up really high as well. You can see where someone goes terribly, horribly wrong in the "charismania" side of the Body and they nearly always have a serious shortage of Wisdom (Fear of the Lord is the BEGINNING of Wisdom) and an excess of some manifestation gift. Maybe they're Prophecy dial is up really high, but they don't know when to keep their mouth shut and not cast pearls before swine. Maybe their Healing dial is up really high but they started making it about THEM instead of giving God the glory. On the other side of the Body we have folks who also don't have enough Fear of the Lord because they think their doctrines are able to perfectly explain God and so they put Him in a box.

Romans 11:29 says that "God's gifts and his call are irrevocable." That means the Gifts are permanent. He'll pour Himself into you, but if you let some of it leak out, you're going to not be balanced as you should be. You'll probably guard carefully the Gift that makes you someone famous, but you'll let leak out the sub-components that made it work within

His purposes and bring Him all the glory – like the wisdom and the discernment and the self-control and the modesty and the humility. You'll keep the flashy stuff and let go of the harder ones that require more maintenance. You can't keep humility and fear of the Lord and self-control if you're not on your knees all the time, keeping your cup full of Jesus daily/hourly.

Some big evangelists that end up in scandal or prison or excess had great big cups and they were all the way full, then they stopped praying and keeping them full and the enemy got in and started messing with them. If you have a cup the size of an oil tanker, just the daily evaporation rate could be tens of thousands of gallons! That much volume filled with sin would shatter the normal person instantly. You better keep your cup full ALL the time! Proverbs 25:26 – "Like a muddied spring or a polluted well is a righteous man who gives way to the wicked." (A well is a really big 'cup'.)

Said again (for emphasis), if you have a candle and you go stand out in the backyard on a summer night, a couple of bugs will come see what's going on. But if God has dialed you up really bright and you're like the halogen arrays on top of a professional football stadium, every bug for MILES is going to come try to smother you! The badness will SWARM on the great big cups and try to crush them any way possible. If you have no openings, they will go for any soft target around you – like your spouse and kids and ministry partners. Smith Wigglesworth, William Branham and John G. Lake all watched their wives die – and then raised them from the dead!

There are people all over the world right now raising the dead and seeing people regrow limbs in front of their eyes and healed of all kinds of terminal illnesses. More of that is coming as soon as the Body starts fully walking in our inheritance and sharing with each other from the abundance of our spirits. Do you want to see God pour out His Spirit on all men? Go find a man and dump out on him all of the Spirit of God that is in you!

You have an endless spring of living water flowing from inside of you, so go point it at somebody and open the faucet all the way! If you have a cup like a shot glass, they may not notice that anything happened. But if you have a cup like an oil tanker and you point a big, fat fire hose at them and crank it on real fast, it will probably knock them down. But PLEASE don't go <u>trying</u> to knock them down for fun, that's just showing off. (And don't put your hand on them and PUSH them down either, that's just witchcraft and manipulation of the worst sort. Please tell God you're sorry for trying to force your will on people and look cool–and pray for more Fear of the Lord while you're at it.)

Are you getting this yet? Let's try another picture.

Know what that is? If you go to church in America, you probably do. Just in case you don't, it's a mixing board for a sound system. All the different dials and buttons and slides control the microphones and sound effects and lighting and all the different things that might be plugged into it. If you don't know what you're doing, you just should NOT be allowed to play with something like this! This is a very valuable piece of equipment and should not be toyed around with! This particular board is a professional model used in recording studios and costs many thousands of dollars. Like my cell phone, it has a great long list of cool features, most of which may never be used for anything. But they're there just in case, just a couple of buttons away.

Every person that you know has a "mixing board" far bigger, far more complicated **and far more valuable** than this one. ONLY the Holy Spirit can manage it. Only God knows what it's true potential and maximum possible range might be. We are like the little kid that peeks into the control room of a nuclear power plant and is awed by the walls of dials and gauges and switches. But you want to be sure not to let a little kid mess with anything in the control center of a nuclear power plant! See the picture. Would YOU want to be in charge of that? If I'm right about this, shouldn't we be putting a WHOLE lot more value on the individuals under our care? Shouldn't we be more careful with their potential?

The variables in play in even a single life are staggeringly massive. Since God sees the end from the beginning, He also knows **all at once** what came before and what is and what is coming. He knows how many souls that kid in your youth group COULD bring into the kingdom, but some or all of them will depend on YOU being obedient and speaking the right word at the right time to that kid. You can't possibly understand the value God places on that kid and the critical importance that you <u>not</u> try to do God's job for Him! You're just going to blow something up.

How can we keep from having more blood on our heads? We are already swimming in guilt and responsibility for all the missed opportunities, disobedience, refusal to share with and care for and love on brethren in need. Not to mention the darkness in the world that's because we didn't take our light out there in sufficient measure. We can't possibly even imagine how many are already going to hell because of the times we didn't do all that we could have. Is that legalism? No, Jesus wants obedience. Why? Because He's the ONLY ONE that can direct our paths so that we don't make things worse and worse all the time. He doesn't want to boss us around and make us miserable! He wants to gently walk us out of the giant bonfire we're standing in the middle of – that we started ourselves! He's the only one that knows the safest possible route out of the fire. It might take a little longer, it might twist and turn and look like we're losing ground, but He knows it's not quite as hot as the direct route that looked good to us but would have killed us instantly.

You see, if a person comes to you and asks for advice about whether to take Job A or Job B and you use all your reason and experience and knowledge and weigh the pro's and con's and help them to decide to take Job B – but that's not what God wanted for them and it wrecks their life – well, that's on your head. It's their fault for listening to you, but it's your fault (especially if you're in a leadership role) for not making sure they were following God and not Man. It could be that you should have just prayed and sought God together and He would have said to turn down both jobs and wait a week because BOTH are decoys from the enemy and Job C is coming and that's the really BIG payoff that was His Perfect Will all along for that person. (Unless you don't think God talks to people, in which case all you've got left is to lean on your own understanding. How's that working for you?)

How many earth-shaking evangelists never launched because we didn't raise them up? How many prophets and apostles and teachers are lost because we had pizza parties and ski trips instead of preaching the power of the Cross? How many people have we filled with the wisdom of man and the ways of the world instead of filling them with Jesus and Faith and Godly Wisdom?

> Colossians 2:8 – *See to it that no one takes you captive through hollow and deceptive philosophy, which depends on human tradition and the basic principles of this world rather than on Christ.*

Paul boasted that the blood of no man was on his head. Wow!! How did he do that? He wrote letters, he traveled all over – he preached until people fell out of windows and died! (But Paul raised him from the dead. Acts 20:7-12) How did he never steer anyone wrong? How did he never make it about him?

Because he always just pointed them toward Jesus. He didn't draw men unto himself, he got behind them and shoved them toward Jesus. He taught relationship and hearing God's voice and obedience to the Spirit in you. He didn't teach obedience to legalism or to systems and structures of man. He didn't seek obedience to Paul, he sought that they obey God alone. I don't want you to even remember me. I just want you to get cleaned out, get a big cup of Jesus, get more fear of the Lord, hear Him really well and then HE will direct your paths. If you let ME direct your paths, you're toast. Don't do it! Take everything here to the Lord and have Him explain it to you and confirm it to you and write it on your heart. Don't take my word for anything.

Ok, sorry. Little detour.

None of the Spiritual Gifts assessments that I have seen take into account all the possible variables. Also, I've never seen one that assumes that everybody has ALL of the Gifts. I'm just sure that if you have ANY Jesus in you, then ALL the Gifts are present. That is, when you get Jesus, all the dials move off of ZERO. Some may never move any higher, but it's there if you need it. That is, I know people that get saved and start hearing God better right away. At first it starts as conviction of sin, but also some zeal and a desire to evangelize. They have more urge to pray and intercede and pray for people that are sick and lost. Some of those prayers get answered. To the degree that they have faith, God continues to pour more into them and dial them up as they are obedient and continue to walk it out and be good stewards of what they have been given. Some people have a big anointing right away for evangelism or prophecy or something, some sneak up on it over time. God can do whatever He wants with your dials. If you don't have, it's because you don't ask – or you got it and didn't use it and it got rusty.

How else can you explain someone that has exceptional wisdom, but only in a given situation. Or someone that can pray healing or miraculous provision down, but only in an emergency. Or people that can heal anything and raise the dead, but only on the mission field? There are times when we "spike" because we're available and willing.

If you don't have a gift, it's because you don't ask. How many times in charismatic congregations does someone come down the aisle seeking the Baptism in the Holy Spirit just so they can speak in tongues? But that's at the BOTTOM of the list of gifts! Paul says to seek the ones at the TOP. I say, seek them ALL! What if you went down the aisle expecting to get them all, begging God to get them all, offering to lay down anything that was in the way so that you could have them all and use them effectively for the Kingdom? Do you think you might get a head start on the person that came down seeking tongues because they just wanted to fit in with everybody else in the youth group?

If you don't have, it's because you don't ask. This is a war between good and evil and we're getting creamed. Why? Because people aren't asking for the really dangerous stuff. The things that really push back the darkness. Particularly wisdom, prophecy, discernment of spirits and interpretation of tongues. In all of my travels around dozens and dozens of congregations (sometimes visiting four or five on one Sunday), I have only RARELY met anyone that has interpretation of tongues and even more rarely people that can see demons. Sadly also, few people that clearly hear the voice of God – and that's not even a Gift of the Spirit! That's just an automatic for ALL believers!

At any moment, God can dial you all the way up and you can do anything that any other brother or sister has ever done. You're just one instant (and a dead body) away from seeing someone raised from the dead. The Jesus in you can do anything, all you have to do is get out of the way and let Him do it through you. You need to get all cleaned out, get your Faith dial turned up really high and know that it's your birthright. Hope to see His glory fill you, do it for the sake of Love and then you'll see the dead raised.

The Master Dials that drive them all are Faith, Hope and Love. But the greatest is Love.

SPECTRUM ANALYSIS OF THE GIFTS

A rainbow has a full spectrum of colors in it. Not just the primary colors, but all kinds of shades in between. Our eyes see the ultraviolet spectrum of light, so we're most familiar with those that we sense, but there are all kinds of other light that our eyes can't see but some animals or scientific instruments can see. Some animals can SEE heat signatures (thermal radiation). We may group a thousand colors in the Yellow or Blue "band" of the rainbow, yet they are all distinct wavelengths if you break them apart.

Again, this is an effort to just get you to see the dizzying complexity of the Holy Spirit and what we all contain. Maybe it's a checklist for you to start asking God for stuff you don't have or to dial you up higher than wherever you are now. Or maybe to seek out or place higher value on some people around you that might have what you are missing.

And when you set yourself to praying that God would dial you up, don't take any man as an example. Don't pray that you would have the anointing of Elisha or the evangelistic power of John the Baptist or the healing anointing of John G. Lake – pray to be like Jesus and then some! He said we would do greater things than He did, so don't put a ceiling on what God might do with you. If He wants you to speak every language on the planet, fine. If He wants you to raise the dead through the internet, fine. Don't box Him in by asking for too little. It's best to just let the Spirit pray through you and He'll ask for the right stuff. If you don't know how to let the Spirit of God pray through you, start by asking for that.

This is by no means exhaustive or definitive. This is just an effort to catalog some of the obvious stuff. There are things coming that we don't and can't even anticipate yet! I'm just trying to show a little sense of how big this really is.

Spectrum Analysis of the Word of Wisdom "Band"

This is not earthly wisdom (that is, book learning), this is Godly wisdom. The pure kernel of raw Truth at the center of everything. Cutting through all the fog and getting right to the heart of the issue in a way that just shocks people because it's so pure. "Cut the baby in half." "Give to Caesar what is Caesars." etc.

Word of Wisdom for the Church

Word of Wisdom for an Individual

Word of Wisdom for your own direction

Rightly dividing the Word of God for teaching – deep calling unto deep

Word of Wisdom for establishment or management of new works

Word of Wisdom for a system of Man – King, Army, Government, etc.

A Word of Wisdom is not the same as wisdom. We can ask for godly wisdom all the time and He gives liberally and without reproach. That's a different dial and tied to the Fear of the Lord dial.

Spectrum Analysis of the Word of Knowledge "Band"

This is knowing something you should not know without supernatural intervention. Like Peter knowing that Ananias and Sapphira had cheated God in Acts 5. Or Jesus knowing how many times the woman at the well had been married or knowing Simon Peter's name. It's not the same as prophecy, but may overlap.

Word of Knowledge about the Church

Word of Knowledge about an individual

Word of Knowledge about the past – something that happened that you wouldn't normally know about

Word of Knowledge about the present – something currently happening, but out of sight

(Future would probably be prophecy.)

An inverse of this band is a spirit of stupor over a person or an army or a nation (or demons). Basically blinding the "eyes" of their mind to the truth of the situation. That is, a removal of knowledge. This is how Richard Wurmbrand was able to smuggle carloads of Bibles into Russia in plain sight in the backseat. Or how the Lord had enemy armies turn on each other and kill themselves. It's knowledge turned inside out. He said that He would even do it to the Jews because they would be ever hearing but never learning. The Lord says that He will shield us and hide us from the eyes of the enemy. We can pray "cloaks" around us when instructed by God that will hide us from the enemy.

Spectrum Analysis of the Faith "Band"

This is not just the ability to believe in Jesus, this is a supernatural ability to endure and be strong. An unshakable belief that God will prevail regardless of outside appearances or the opinion of ANYONE.

This is a dial from SOME supernatural faith and strength to a deepset supernatural faith so strong that you can preach Jesus while burning at the stake; that you can believe God is going to raise the dead every time even though you've prayed 1,000 times on dead people and it hasn't happened yet; that NO MATTER WHAT, God will answer you. The Apostle Paul had a KNOWING that even if shipwrecked, not a single person would be lost; or if bitten by a snake it wouldn't hurt him. He KNEW when he cursed a king's magician that the guy would instantly go blind exactly like Paul said. Paul knew that he would be arrested, imprisoned and eventually killed if he went back to Jerusalem, but He knew it was God's plan to get him before kings and emperors and that it would be fine.

Faith is embedded in the middle because it drives all the others. All the gifts should be used in accordance with the measure of Faith you have. So whatever else you have, pray for more Faith and more Wisdom.

Spectrum Analysis of the Healings "Band"

Essentially a gift of intercession, this also carries with it authority to affect changes in the natural or spiritual realms. This can range from local (laying hands on) to long distance. From healing a headache to regrowing limbs or raising the dead (which would probably require physical, mental, emotional and spiritual all at once!).

Anointing for physical healings – restoration or replacement of physical damage or affliction.

Anointing for mental healings – mangled thought processes or mistaken views, probably demonic.

Anointing for emotional healings – hurts and pains and lack of peace, bitterness, abuse.

Anointing for spiritual healings – deliverance/exorcism from spiritual oppressions.

Anointing for creative healings – remaking something not there (limb regrown, new brain cells, new organ, etc.)

Anointing for healings of groups – families, congregations, races, specific victims of some sort, cities, states, nations

This may also include the reverse. That is, actually CAUSING illness (leprosy, blindness, death, etc.). Lots of people in the Bible spoke curses that removed healing over people or nations. That may be a healing dial or it may be under prophecy or miracles (or all). Either way, you better be REALLY, REALLY careful with that one!! It's just a VERY fine line away from witchcraft – and God really hates witchcraft! DO NOT even speak something like that unless you specifically hear God tell you to! If you have a lot of authority in healing or prophecy, the words you speak have power and you need to be very careful.

Spectrum Analysis of the Workings of Miracles "Band"

These are things that bend or outright violate what we normally think are the laws of nature. Since God made them, He knows how to get around the rules. It's a miracle because it is outside of what would be possible without supernatural intervention - iron just doesn't float, people just don't instantly drop dead when you tell them to, armies don't just kill themselves for no reason, the oil in a jar should run out sooner or later, a man cannot outrun a team of horses, you just can't feed that many people with five loaves and two fishies, you can't just declare a drought and the rain stops, etc. And yet, all of these things happened and still can when God commands it through an obedient man.

Miraculous provision (money, food, water, etc.)

Miraculous protection (shields, cloaks of stupor, blindness, angels, poisons, etc.)

Miraculous movement (theoportation – Acts 8:39-40, super speed – I Kings 18:44-46, etc.)

Miraculous movement of objects (theokinesis – 2 Kings 6:1-7)

Miraculous weather responses (storms quieted, drought, flood, wind, rain, etc.)

Miraculous responses by nature (wild animals – 2 Kings 2:23-25; trees, plants, springs, wells)

Miraculous planetary responses (sun going backwards or standing still, earthquakes)

Spectrum Analysis of the Prophecy "Band"

Not the same as the "Calling" of Prophet. MANY people can and should prophecy either to each other or to the world, but the OFFICE of Prophet is different. Since Jesus IS the Spirit of Prophecy and we all have Jesus, we should all prophecy to some degree or another. If you have Jesus, your prophecy dial is AUTOMATICALLY not on Zero. You may think it's just intuition or deja vu, but it's Jesus. You may think it's just a weird dream, but it could be Jesus. (But not always.) Even if you just speak forth something from God's word but with divine conviction, that's prophecy.

Message to the Church

Message to an individual

Message to king, government, army, etc.

Rightly dividing the Word of God and speaking forth the Logos

Seeing otherwise hidden past of an individual or group

Seeing otherwise hidden present of an individual or group

Seeing future of an individual or group

Speaking forth demanding instant action (Raise up dry bones! Waves be still!)

God directly speaking through you in first person

God dictating to you (or divinely inspiring) a message in writing

Dreams, closed visions (eyes closed), open visions (eyes open)

(I suspect that interpretation of dreams and visions is a part of the Wisdom band.)

Spectrum Analysis of the Discernment of Spirits "Band"

This is being able to see in the spirit and to tell the difference between the good guys and the bad guys. The more of this you have, the more the door opens between the natural and the spiritual and you can see in both places at the same time and discern who is for you and who is against you. The Wisdom band is really important here because you need to hear God really well before you act on anything that you see. The higher your dial here, the more reliability, clarity and resolution you get to all the senses. These are watchmen and advance scouts and snipers that can see the enemy a long way away and identify troop movements and pick off infiltrators. We need LOTS more of these.

A vague sense that someone is "not quite right"

A general sense that a place has strongholds or evil present

A truth-detector that reliably tells you when someone is lying or not from God.

Clearly seeing demons in the "spirit" (hearing, smelling, tasting, feeling)

Clearly seeing demons in the "natural" with open eyes (hearing, smelling, tasting, feeling)

Clearly seeing principalities or powers over places or cities or nations

Seeing angels or other things of heaven in the "spirit" (hearing, smelling, tasting, feeling)

Summoning and directing ministering angels to the degree of authority and faith granted

(Cloaking so as to be hidden from the spiritual eyes of the enemy – or even friends – is probably an inverse of this band. Some other things like praying "hedges" or shields of protection may also require a Discernment Gift to see and operate most effectively. Anybody can pray a shield, but not everybody can SEE them, manage them, reinforce them and clean them out if breached.)

Spectrum Analysis of the Giving "Band"

This is a supernatural ability to give of oneself. This is NOT tithing or some token giving. This is supernaturally powered sacrificial giving. It's not about the quantity, it's about the sacrifice and the spirit behind it.

Giving of material resources

Giving of mental resources

Giving of emotional resources

Giving of spiritual resources

(Pouring your cup out is Giving. Pouring it out fully and sacrificially is BIG Giving. Pouring it out eternally is maximum giving.)

Spectrum Analysis of the Helps "Band"

This is a supernatural ability to help those in need. This is not helping a little, this is supernatural helping in just the right way at just the right time beyond what seems reasonable to someone not so motivated.

Giving of time resources

Giving of physical resources/labor

Spectrum Analysis of the Mercy "Band"

This is a supernatural ability to feel for those in need. To see people through the eyes of Jesus and to cry when He cries and laugh when He laughs, to forgive as He forgives. This is empathy of the highest Godly order. This is love.

Mercy, empathy and love for individuals, families, congregations, nations, the world.

Spectrum Analysis of the Administration "Band"

A supernatural ability to direct the flow of people, money, goods, services, information, time, etc.

Coordinating efforts of others toward a common goal.

Efficient, selfless networking with Giving, Helps, Mercy, Prophecy, and other bands toward an efficient delivery of goods, services, mercy, evangelism, communication or other.

Spectrum Analysis of the Exhortation "Band"

A supernatural ability to be encouraging and say the affirming, uplifting word that is needed at just the right moment. May involve lots of hugging.

Spectrum Analysis of the Tongues "Band"

Basically it's allowing the Holy Spirit to prophecy or speak through you in whatever way He wants. It may or may not be linguistic. I'm aware of people speaking in other languages of men, but there are also other options in this "band".

Languages of Man – Many options or frequencies

Languages of Angels – Many options or frequencies

Groaning/Travail (Romans 8, Ezek 21)

Tears/Weeping

Specific Purpose Tongues – Intercession, Miracles, Praise, Warfare, etc.

Communication (with Headquarters) Tongues

Singing in Tongues

Inspired playing of instruments

Inspired body movement - dance

Other prophetic physical or physiological responses that are "decent and in order"

Interpretation of Tongues

Some of these overlap with Prophecy if they are interpreted.

Some don't necessarily need interpretation – like dance, music, groaning, weeping, etc.

Some of these may just be conglomerations of other dials, but they seem to be things that can be poured out, even though they have an influence on a bunch of other things and may not really be independent. I know that may not fully make sense, but God is really complicated and the best we can do sometimes is write down what we observe, even if we don't understand the mechanics of it or the scriptural justification for it.

Other Dials that we've observed:

Wisdom (not Word of Wisdom)

Fear of the Lord (actually a flavor of Wisdom)

Peace (may actually be a flavor of Faith)

Strength (may actually be a flavor of Faith)

Patience (may actually be a flavor of Faith)

Authority (for a specific work – delegation/commissioning type thing)

CAN YOU PRAY THE HARD PRAYER?

The Lord gave me a really simple understanding of the nature of the warfare we endure. It goes like this – the point of this life is to raise up big strong brothers and sisters for Jesus. The Father wants big, spiritually muscle-bound warriors, not soft couch potatoes. You can't build up muscle without breaking it down first. You need resistance training. Without something to push against, you can't build muscle.

So it's like I'm on the bench press and satan is the barbell and the struggles and problems and cares of life are the weights. The Lord said that He would never let it go too far.

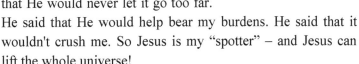

He said that He would help bear my burdens. He said that it wouldn't crush me. So Jesus is my "spotter" – and Jesus can lift the whole universe!

So, satan is just the tool used for resistance training, right? So he can't go beyond what the Lord allows and it's all just to make me big and strong? And Jesus is my spotter? When I wear out, He's going to pick it up?

Well, then, Lord, put **ALL** the weights on and let's go!! Let's get this over with! I don't care how much it hurts, put all the weight on and get me big and strong really fast! There's a war between good and evil and I think we're losing. I could lift 50 pounds and I'd never break a sweat or be the least big inconvenienced. But I'm never going to build muscle either! So put 1000 pounds on and let's go! You know what I can handle and you'll help when I'm weak. In fact, You get MORE glory when I'm weak, so put SO MUCH weight on it that I could never possibly lift it without You! Then everybody will know it was a miracle and I won't get any of the credit! Yeah, that's what I want. Load me up. I don't care how much it hurts, I don't care how much I whine and complain, You are my Personal Trainer so don't let up. No matter how annoying I am and how many times I ask You to take the weight off, don't do it! Finish what You started in me and let's get it over with so I can be fully ready to go serve Your Body in the biggest, best possible way.

Wanna pray that? I can promise you it's going to hurt – a LOT. (Read the Warning Label again.) He will ABSOLUTELY take you seriously and all kinds of really horrifyingly hard things are going to start pretty much immediately. You need to figure that NOTHING in your life is safe from that prayer. Not family, not job, not health, not even your calling or your gifts. He might not even feed you. It might mean prison, it might even mean ending up on crack and sleeping under a bridge is necessary to burn everything out of you and prepare you for HIS perfect plan for your life. He's very creative. And He is the only one that can know what it's going to take. But I can promise you this, He is a good Dad and He's never going to push it beyond what is absolutely necessary. He's never going to spank you one extra time just cause it makes Him feel good. The more you embrace the refining fire, the easier it will be.

I'm speaking from personal experience here. There is no prayer that will get you ready for war faster, but there's no prayer that will hurt more either. But if you're so full of Jesus that nothing else can fit, you won't care too much about the pain. And it's really fun to watch Him lifting when you can't do it anymore. This is maximum adrenalin praying.

Don't blame me for whatever comes. You've been properly warned. Now, if you're willing, pray this.

Dear Lord Jesus, I trust You. I know You'll get me through. I want to be fully equipped, fully armored, fully broken and fully willing to do your perfect will. Whatever in me that is resisting You – kill it with prejudice. Lord, there is a monster inside of me and it's me. Hunt it down and kill it and hang its head on the wall of my heart so I'll never forget what I was. Put all the weight on. Load me up. Whatever it takes, I trust You. I'm ready now, Lord. Do it right now! I know this prayer is inside Your will, so I know You are going to answer it. Just please don't ever leave me. In the mighty name of my Lord Jesus Christ, Amen.

I Peter 4:12-14 – *Beloved, think it not strange concerning the fiery trial which is to try you, as though some strange thing happened unto you: If ye be reproached for the name of Christ, happy [are ye]; for the spirit of glory and of God resteth upon you: on their part he is evil spoken of, but on your part he is glorified.*

2 Corinthians 4:17 – *For our light affliction, which is but for a moment, worketh for us a far more exceeding [and] eternal weight of glory;*

Hebrews 11:25 – *Choosing rather to suffer affliction with the people of God, than to enjoy the pleasures of sin for a season*

Luke 6:22-23 – *Blessed are ye, when men shall hate you, and when they shall separate you [from their company], and shall reproach [you], and cast out your name as evil, for the Son of man's sake. Rejoice ye in that day, and leap for joy: for, behold, your reward [is] great in heaven: for in the like manner did their fathers unto the prophets.*

OK, SO HOW DO YOU POUR OUT YOUR CUP?

If you skipped straight to this chapter and missed all the stuff before – GO BACK!!! This ain't a game. I'm not kidding around here. If you don't have the proper foundation on which to build this, you'll make a giant mess!! No peeking!! Start at the front.

Well, here's the thing. I think it's just rightly dividing the Word of God to illustrate about *charisma* and *dunamis* and about the examples of impartation of the Holy Spirit and of Gifts by the apostles and others. I think we're safe by encouraging people to pour themselves out and showing the Biblical requirement to do so and the obvious deficit of it in the Church. But I don't want to establish some artificial procedural doctrine. The last thing we need in the Church are more programs and curriculums and people preaching that theirs is the only way! I think there are some universal principles in play here, but I'm just really hesitant to set some kind of policy about how the mechanics of it should work.

There are some things that we know. The actual physical contact of the laying on of hands was important and a common element in the Bible. Not just for the commissioning of missionaries, but for healing and for receiving the empowering of the Holy Spirit and for impartation of Gifts. But, sometimes people were healed without anyone touching them, so it's not an absolute. Nobody laid hands on the disciples in the upper room (well, God did). Sometimes contact reinforces faith and is necessary for the recipient, sometimes it's not required. Lots of examples of people being told what to do to be healed, and as they obeyed they were made well.

I can only tell you what the Holy Spirit taught me about this. Your own experience may be substantially different and I'm not going to tell you it's wrong if there is clear fruit. I'm not trying to make clones of me, you do whatever the Lord shows you. Just get everything out of the way and hear Him really well.

I'm going to be really transparent here because at this point, I've got nothing to lose anyway. I didn't get to the "cup model" as some theoretical construct, God started showing me my cup and that's what it looked like. I'd wake up every morning and ask Him how full my cup was and I'd spend time with Him until I was sure my cup was all the way full. Throughout the day, as I could feel (or see) it drain off, I would make sure and get time with Him and drink from the river of life. I wasn't always good at it, but He has taught me a lot as I've grown in Christ.

I would talk to other people about it and encourage them to ask the Lord to show them their own cup. Other people started seeing their cups and they looked just the same as what I was seeing (red, yellow and blue). People who had never even seen the graphic were describing it to me the same way! Over and over I would show the model to someone and ask them if they wanted to get the SIN out and get a big cup of Jesus, even if it hurt. They would agree and then I would pray for them and ask the Lord to pour any good thing in my cup into theirs. If I put my hand on someone, I would feel the Spirit moving through my arm and hand and vibrating like when you hold a gas pump at the gas station. When they were full, it would just shut off. If I tried to "push" it would go faster but I could NOT push more into somebody that was full (or push something that God said He didn't want them to have).

Over and over I watched people get filled with the Holy Spirit this way. Sometimes they would speak in tongues, sometimes they wouldn't – or sometimes later on. I didn't care to push them about that gift because I didn't need it as "initial evidence" because the Lord just let me actually <u>watch</u> their cup get full! What do I need flesh and blood proof for? We're to see in the spirit anyway and I watched them get filled. And the evidence that they got full was that it often turned their life upside down right away. If they got a lot bigger cup and learned how to keep it full, they often started going through all kinds of amazing adventures as the enemy right away tried to slow them down. As you'd expect, some gave in and some stood strong. The ones that did the best were the ones that could receive in faith and learned how to keep their cup full all the time. The ones that had the most child-like faith were always the ones that did the best. Those that want to drink in Jesus all the time, all day long.

Most often it didn't do much good to fill someone's cup if they had all kinds of entrenched bad stuff that had effectively "corked" their cup. The springs of living water were capped because of the embedded SIN and strongholds and strategies of the enemy that needed to be purged first. So we would talk about what might be in their cup that shouldn't and if they didn't know right away what it was that was holding them back from the fullness of God, we'd pray and God would often tell me what the strongholds were in their life. Then I would tell them, they would cry (because nobody was supposed to know about that so it must be God), then they would repent, we'd rebuke it in the name of Jesus and get their cup full. Lots of people got healed of spiritual and physical illnesses at the same time by this process.

I've learned that I can pour my cup out on people remotely through intercessory prayer, online discussion boards, phone calls, or from across a room. I've learned that if your cup is big enough, you can pour it out on a whole congregation. Sometimes the Lord sends me to a congregation just to sit quietly in the back and pray that the worship team or the leadership or the whole congregation would be filled as full as He'll allow. If you have a really, really big cup, you can fill a whole town. I think that's what Paul did when he went into a town and interceded for them collectively and offered himself up for them all. I think that's what Daniel Nash did for Charles Finney. (Do a Google search for Daniel Nash or Father Nash and read about this amazing man!)

I think you can see Moses and Paul pouring out their entire eternal cups on a whole race (Ex. 32:32, Rom. 9:22-23) Jesus had a cup so big, He could pour it out on all people for all time. In fact, He poured Himself out and allowed the SIN of all people to be poured into a cup that had never had SIN in it before. He stood in the gap for us and took on all our icky ugliness. He prayed the prayer of Moses for everybody ever. And unlike Moses, He had the authority to do it on a global scale.

In fact, Jesus had a cup so big that He could fill everybody's cup for all time SO full that it would be like an endless stream of living water flowing up from inside of you. That is, those who acknowledge Him and who He is and what He did and are willing to receive from Him will be able to get there cup so full that nothing else will fit and, if they're obedient with it, can pour it out on others so freely that it will never run out. His cup is still being poured out on us all the time. The only limitation to how much you can be filled with Him and His Spirit is the degree to which you are willing to receive it and lay down anything that is in the way. Isn't that the coolest thing ever!?! Kind of changes the whole nature of "church" doesn't it?

Can it really be that simple? Well, believe in faith and give it a try. I have seen so much evidence and confirmation of this that I don't even doubt it for a second anymore. I've seen people just LIGHT UP and become fierce faith-walking warriors when you get them unclogged, pray the hard prayer and get them full of Jesus. Then their cup just keeps getting bigger and bigger the more they listen to Him and obey.

But please, remember the warning, the enemy is going to do EVERYTHING possible to slow you down, to plant fear and doubt, to get you to deny that this is real. He won't be able to win on scriptural grounds, but some religious spirit will try really hard to get you to either deny all of this or to stop walking in it once you start. Expect resistance!! Be ready for it. DO NOT underestimate it!

He that is in you is bigger, greater, stronger, older, smarter, and more patient and loving than he that is in the world. Let Him do the fighting for you. This isn't about you anyway.

ARE YOU SURE YOU'RE NOT NUTS?

Boy, I'll tell you what! Sometimes I read over stuff like this that I have written and the Missouri Show-Me, Southern Baptist preacher's kid in me does sort of wonder if I'm nuts. But the Word of God is clear, we are spiritual beings temporarily trapped in jars of clay. We are to walk in the spirit, not focus on the flesh. Our battle is NOT against flesh and blood, but against powers and principalities and wickedness in high places and the dark forces of this world. Neither is our battle to be done WITH our flesh and blood. Our spirit (or rather His in us) is where our true power rests.

So, yeah, this seems really supernatural and mystical to me sometimes, except that God has proven it to me so many times that I couldn't even begin to count. I've seen demons (in the spirit) on someone and reached out and grabbed them and ripped them off and they quit smoking or are healed of Autism or their pain stops instantly or they don't need their schizophrenia medicine anymore. Over and over and over.

And I've seen people (strong Christians!) be unable or unwilling to keep the doors shut and it comes back seven times worse and within HOURS they're beating their wife and doing drugs and cursing me out – or worse! I know demons are real because the Lord has proven it to me over and over and I've seen what they do, how they act, where they hide, how to get rid of them, how they come back, how they work together and more.

There is a certain segment of the "church" that will insult and demean anything that is "supernatural" and yet they gather together to pray on Wednesday nights for the sick people in their churches. They pray that the doctors would have wisdom, that their recovery would be slightly faster than normal, that they would have peace with the sickness that the Lord has placed on them. Hogwash! What kind of power is that? What kind of inheritance? If you don't believe God heals, then why pray at all? Why not just write a note of encouragement to their doctor? If you just sit around and send out good vibes to their doctor, how is that not a form of New Age meditation? Where in the Bible does it say to go to a doctor anyway? Who is the Great Physician? What doctor can heal if God doesn't want someone healed? What doctor can save a life that God wants to take? And who can kill someone God wants to keep alive? How many examples do you want of people that I know that are unkillable? I have a friend that tried to commit suicide so many times and kept getting saved by angels that finally an angel came and said, "Would you just KNOCK IT OFF! We're never going to let you kill yourself!" And that was BEFORE he came to Jesus! If God has something for you to do, until you do it, you're indestructible! Why be afraid of Man? And if God wants you dead, NOBODY can save you. Be afraid of God.

Oops! Sorry, started preaching again. Anyway ...

Those sections of the church that deny that the Gifts of the Spirit are for today are still brothers and sisters and I love them. But they're not going to be very much help fighting a war in the spirit with weapons they say aren't real and against an enemy they insist isn't there. Some even believe that God doesn't speak to people anymore. What kind of a war is that? In the meantime, their churches are full of sick, shackled, addicted, fearful, obese people with no peace and joy and victory. They have the appearance of Christ, but deny the power thereof. That can't be good. But I love them and want them to come around. It's not the people's fault, it's the doctrines of man jammed down their throat by seminarians who will not back down from the status quo. But I think God is coming in power real soon and He's going to settle the issue once and for all.

Yes, there are lying signs and wonders already and many more coming. There are false prophets that heal and deliver people of demons (or seem to). But the fact that satan has cheap imitations DOES NOT negate the originals! Who benefits most if God does supernatural stuff and satan does supernatural stuff, but you dismiss them BOTH because ONE of them was from satan? Don't you think that's going to irritate God – to constantly be told that anything supernatural that He does was actually the work of satan? I mean how can God do anything that's NOT supernatural – by definition, He's not "natural"! When God equips someone with faith and power and they take the Bible seriously and go out and fulfill the Great Commission as it's written at the end of the Gospel of Mark and people keep saying they are tools of satan, don't you think that's going to irritate God?

Whatever else I may be, I've got peace and joy and victory and I'm deliriously happy. If the voice I'm hearing is NOT God, then it sure sounds like Him and He keeps telling me to do stuff that you would think would really, really make satan mad. If this voice isn't really God, I don't care, I'm gonna stick with it until this whole ride plays out to the end. I'm going to bet on radical obedience and a pure heart being a really good thing (heavenly treasure-wise) and if I go down, I'm going down swinging for the fences. God will judge my heart, not the perfection and purity of my doctrine.

So, if I'm crazy, don't medicate me, I'm really enjoying it.

HOW WOULD THIS REALLY CHANGE
THE CHURCH?

I don't know if you really see the impact of all of this, but if I'm right, then it really changes everything. If you can pour out your spirit, then we'll do a lot less filling their brains and a lot more filling their spirit. If people in the congregations were fully equipped with the gift of discernment and were aware of who had a deficit or had things clogging them up, it would make every single member a potential minister. It would empower every member to reach out and help every other. And it would be hard to make it about their knowledge or their anointing or their diploma, because there might be little kids with bigger cups of Jesus!

Other stuff that might change? There'd be a whole lot less brain training and a whole lot more fellowshiping and sharing and breaking bread and investing in each other. There would be a whole lot more people spiritually armored up and ready to take on the darkness of this world. There would be a whole lot less budget needs and if the government took all our buildings and overhead projectors away, nobody would care because you can pour your cup out on somebody and worship in a park or a cave or an office building. You know, it might just disrupt the entire infrastructure of the entire institutional church system. I wonder what kind of chaos that might cause to people that don't want to give up their old wineskins?

It would also take the emphasis off of a "senior pastor" and shift the responsibility of eldership to where it should be – to those who have the biggest cup of Jesus. It would value people for their spiritual assets – for their Biblical Fruit, not for their degrees or speaking ability or their new book deal or any other measure. The little old lady in the walker or the kid in Sunday School might be the one people seek out when they need prayer. If the pastor wants to stay in the lead, then he's going to have to work hard to make sure that he pours himself out all the time and keeps his cup bigger than anybody else's. For that matter, why does he need to be in the lead? Why not just direct the resources of the assembly toward meeting needs and try not to make it about him. That would be nice.

But you can't grow if you have embedded sin that you're unwilling to get out. Your spring of living water can't flow from inside of you if you've got it corked with badness. Before we can really get this show on the road, we need to help individuals get unplugged and then we need to step back and take a look at the cup of our assembly and see what we need to do to get it unplugged as well.

This isn't theory. I've seen this work. I've been in a fellowship where everyone there had been through this, had been fully cleaned out, was walking in holiness, had giant cups of Jesus and really, REALLY knew how to love on each other like Jesus. I can tell you, it's as far from the institutional, systematized churches as the East is from the West. It's pure and beautiful and as close to heaven as I've ever found on earth! Fellowship is purer, everyone shares with each as they have a need – body, soul and spirit. The Holy Spirit flows like a mighty river and it's pure and clean and deep. The best "church service" I've ever been to was an amazing 2 ½ hours of prophetic worship, repentance, anointing and communion led entirely and seamlessly by the Spirit of God through a seven year old girl! And that was not in a big sanctuary – that was in a furniture store!

Have you ever been in a group of people that trusted God completely for everything and knew how to love each other like Christ loves the Church? People that would NOT leave a need unmet, no matter what it cost them? I want nothing more than to see that in every body of believers everywhere. I'm pouring myself out daily toward that goal. And I believe that is what is coming, as soon as people learn how to be fully free, fully equipped, fully sacrificial – that is, get full of Jesus and stay full.

Let's try this a different way. Proverbs 3:5-10 lays it out pretty clearly.

IF YOU:

5 Trust in the LORD with all your heart
TRUST HIM WITH ALL

and lean not on your own understanding;
LEAN ON NONE OF YOUR OWN UNDERSTANDING

6 in all your ways acknowledge him,
LISTEN REAL GOOD

and he will make your paths straight.
LET HIM GUIDE <u>ALL</u> YOUR PATHS

7 Do not be wise in your own eyes;
KILL PRIDE

fear the LORD
SEEK WISDOM

and shun evil.
SEEK RIGHTEOUSNESS

8 This will bring health to your body
PHYSICALLY & SPIRITUALLY, PERSONALLY & COLLECTIVELY

and nourishment to your bones.
TRUE MEAT, NOT JUST MILK

9 Honor the LORD with your wealth,
SPIRITUAL WEALTH <u>AND</u> MATERIAL WEALTH

with the firstfruits of all your crops;
SHARE YOUR BEST WITH THOSE IN NEED AS HE DIRECTS

10 **<u>THEN</u>** your **barns** will be **filled** to **overflowing**, and your **vats** will **brim over** with **new wine**.

A barn is a big storage place for lots of smaller containers - essentially the church! When the Church starts working like THIS, then all of the "vats" of their people will brim over and the barns themselves will be filled to overflowing.

(Did you notice how similar this is to the Beatitudes we talked about before?) Want some more verses to confirm it?

1 Thes. 4:4 – *That every one of you should know how to posses his vessel in sanctification and honour;*

2 Timothy 2:20-26 – *20 But in a great house there are not only <u>vessels</u> of gold and silver, but also of wood and earthenware, and some for honorable and noble [use] and some for menial and ignoble [use]. 21 So whoever cleanses himself [from what is ignoble and unclean, who separates himself from contact with contaminating and corrupting influences] will [then himself] be a <u>vessel</u> set apart and useful for honorable and noble purposes, consecrated and profitable to the Master, fit and ready for any good work. 22 Shun youthful lusts and flee from them, and aim at and pursue righteousness (all that is virtuous and good, right living, conformity to the will of God in thought, word, and deed); [and aim at and pursue] faith, love, [and] peace (harmony and concord with others) in fellowship with all [Christians], who call upon the Lord out of a pure heart. 23 But refuse (shut your mind against, have nothing to do with) trifling (ill-informed, unedifying, stupid) controversies over ignorant questionings, for you know that they foster strife and breed quarrels. 24 And the servant of the Lord must not be quarrelsome (fighting and contending). Instead, he must be kindly to everyone and mild-tempered [preserving the bond of peace]; he must be a skilled and suitable teacher, patient and forbearing and willing to suffer wrong. 25 He must correct his opponents with courtesy and gentleness, in the hope that God may grant that they will repent and come to know the Truth [that they will perceive and recognize and become accurately acquainted with and acknowledge it], 26 And that they may come to their senses [and] escape out of the*

194

snare of the devil, having been held captive by him, [henceforth] to do His [God's] will.

Could it be any more clear than that? Whether it's you individually or the "cup" of your congregation, your town or your country – get the nasty, useless goo out of your cup!! You are **NOT** going to be "set apart and useful for honorable and noble purposes, consecrated and profitable to the Master, fit and ready for any good work" **UNTIL** you are cleansed!

What is it that we are SUPPOSED to be doing? Here's the list:

- Shun lusts and flee from them.

- Aim at and pursue righteousness, virtuous and good, right living.

- Conforming to the will of the Lord in thought, word and deed.

- Pursue faith, love and peace in fellowship with all who call upon the Lord out of a pure heart.

- Refuse trifling controversies over ignorant questionings that foster strife and breed quarrels.

- Do not be quarrelsome.

- Be kindly to everyone and mild-tempered

- Be a skilled and suitable teacher, patient and forbearing and willing to suffer wrong.

- Correct opponents with courtesy and gentleness, in hope that GOD will straighten them out.

- In hope that they will escape the rulers that hold them captive, so that they can do His will.

Does that look much like the church system we currently have in place? Did we get 37,000+ denominations by doing the stuff on this list? Hmmm. I wonder if God's really happy about this mess?

Need another one? How about Romans 12?

> 1 *I appeal to you therefore, brethren, and beg of you in view of [all] the mercies of God, to make a decisive dedication of your bodies [presenting all your members and faculties] as a living sacrifice, holy (devoted, consecrated) and well pleasing to God, which is your reasonable (rational, intelligent) service and spiritual worship.*

Present your bodies as living sacrifices. What body? Your physical body? Yes. Your family? Yes. Your congregation? Yes. Your nation? Yes. Why? Because it is your minimum reasonable service to the God of the universe whom you worship. What do we have to do before we offer the sacrifice? Make sure it is holy – cleaned out, washed off and worthy so that it is well pleasing to God. Don't think that a one-eyed lamb or a bull with three legs is going to do! Don't offer half of your body – wash it clean and put the WHOLE thing up on the altar and lay there. Don't hold back.

> 2 *Do not be conformed to this world (this age), [fashioned after and adapted to its external, superficial customs], but be transformed (changed) by the [entire] renewal of your mind [by its new ideals and its new attitude], so that you may prove [for yourselves] what is the good and acceptable and perfect will of God, even the thing which is good and acceptable and perfect [in His sight for you].*

If you offer your body as a living sacrifice, He is going to then perform these three simple steps. This is God's three step plan to restore the Body. First, He's going to fix it so you stop conforming to the world. Laying naked on an altar and waiting for someone to sacrifice you is a good start. Then, when He's good and ready, He's going to cut your head off and graft His head on. He will reboot you back to the defaults and re-NEW your mind – back the way it was when it was before the viruses of the world messed it all up – that is, He'll make it like Christ. THEN you will know what is the good and acceptable and perfect will of God. Until you do those three steps you're just going to have to guess at what His will is. As long as you're conforming to the world you <u>can't</u> get your mind renewed and you <u>won't</u> know what He really wants for you. Forget spending forty days on purpose to figure out what you can do for God, it's not going to do <u>any</u> good until you stop conforming to the world. The Word of God says so.

> 3 *For by the grace (unmerited favor of God) given to me I warn everyone among you not to estimate and think of himself more highly than he ought [not to have an exaggerated opinion of his own importance], but to rate his ability with sober judgment, each according to the degree of faith apportioned by God to him.*

Kill pride. Seek Wisdom. Judge rightly.

> 4 *For as in one physical body we have many parts (organs, members) and all of these parts do not have the same function or use,*

Get that? Not everybody can be toes or eyeballs. Diversity is good. Stop cloning people to be just like you instead of letting them be who God created them to be. We need all the parts doing what they were made for, not trying to be something they're not.

> 5 *So we, numerous as we are, are one body in Christ (the Messiah) and individually we are parts one of another [mutually dependent on one another].*

If you think you can do without all the other parts, you're wrong. This is a multi-part harmony that He wrote, not thousands of people all singing the melody line in unison.

> 6 *Having gifts (faculties, talents, qualities) that differ according to the grace given us, let us use them: [He whose gift is] prophecy, [let him prophesy] according to the proportion of his faith;*

Remember, this word "gifts" is "charisma" - he's talking about spiritual gifts, each used according the quantity of grace and faith of each. But they are not for show, they're to be used!

> 7 *[He whose gift is] practical service, let him give himself to serving; he who teaches, to his teaching; 8 He who exhorts (encourages), to his exhortation; he who contributes, let him do it in simplicity and liberality; he who gives aid and superintends, with zeal and singleness of mind; he who does acts of mercy, with genuine cheerfulness and joyful eagerness.*

Whatever God gave you, use it with love and sincerity. If God gave you a weapon and you let it lay around, it's just going to get rusty. Take it out to the range and practice with it until you're a sharpshooter. Get so good that you can shoot the wings off a fly at a thousand yards.

9 [Let your] love be sincere (a real thing); hate what is evil [loathe all ungodliness, turn in horror from wickedness], but hold fast to that which is good. 10 Love one another with brotherly affection [as members of one family], giving precedence and showing honor to one another. 11 Never lag in zeal and in earnest endeavor; be aglow and burning with the Spirit, serving the Lord. 12 Rejoice and exult in hope; be steadfast and patient in suffering and tribulation; be constant in prayer. 13 Contribute to the needs of God's people [sharing in the necessities of the saints]; pursue the practice of hospitality. 14 Bless those who persecute you [who are cruel in their attitude toward you]; bless and do not curse them. 15 Rejoice with those who rejoice [sharing others' joy], and weep with those who weep [sharing others' grief]. 16 Live in harmony with one another; do not be haughty (snobbish, high-minded, exclusive), but readily adjust yourself to [people, things] and give yourselves to humble tasks. Never overestimate yourself or be wise in your own conceits. 17 Repay no one evil for evil, but take thought for what is honest and proper and noble [aiming to be above reproach] in the sight of everyone. 18 If possible, as far as it depends on you, live at peace with everyone. 19 Beloved, never avenge yourselves, but leave the way open for [God's] wrath; for it is written, Vengeance is Mine, I will repay (requite), says the Lord.

Be real. Hate evil. Be good. Love your brothers and sisters no matter what. Step back and promote them instead of yourselves. Look on the bright side. Hang in there no matter what storms come. Pray all the time. Share with people when they need something. Share your stuff cheerfully. Be nice, even to bullies. When someone laughs, laugh with them, when they cry, cry with them. Play nice and don't pick favorites. Be willing to do the dirty chores. Don't be arrogant. Don't be mean. Think good thoughts. Try to get along with everybody. Don't hit back, let God fix the bullies. He'll take care of them.

20 But if your enemy is hungry, feed him; if he is thirsty, give him drink; for by so doing you will heap burning coals upon his head.

Instead of doing what the world expects, now that you don't conform to the world anymore, do the crazy thing. The people that are the most against you, feed them and care for them and pour out onto them. You know what will happen? It will drive them nuts. And if they want to get out from under the burning coals of conviction, the only way to do it is to stop being an enemy.

21 Do not let yourself be overcome by evil, but overcome (master) evil with good.

If you can do this stuff, you'll win. If not, you're toast.

HOW DO WE GET OUR CORPORATE
CUP CLEANED OUT?

How do you implement this in a whole congregation? First, you need to understand that revival and restoration is NOT going to come until you say you're sorry for being the kind of people that need reviving in the first place. You have to say you're sorry for blowing out the <u>last</u> pillar of fire that He sent! Here in Kansas City, God has been trying to get revivals going for 200+ years and we keep getting in His way. Why is He going to trust you with another move of God when you keep making it about YOU and tearing each other to shreds when it comes? You're going to have to cleanse the temple before the glory cloud will come back. That means individually and collectively taking out the trash.

What do you do when the locusts have come and eaten everything? When the land has stopped producing and the sheep and the cattle mill around looking for green pasture and can't find any?

In the first twelve verses of Joel chapter 1 we see a description of and lamenting for the land that has been devastated. Particularly verse 4: (NIV)

What the locust swarm has left the great locusts have eaten; what the great locusts have left the young locusts have eaten; what the young locusts have left other locusts have eaten.

These are the ultimate consumers. They have devoured everything that is useful and left nothing behind.

Then the solution is proposed in verse 13 and 14:

Put on sackcloth, O priests, and mourn; wail, you who minister before the altar. Come, spend the night in sackcloth, you who minister before my God; for the grain offerings and drink offerings are withheld from the house of your God. Declare a holy fast; call a sacred assembly. Summon the elders and all who live in the land to the house of the LORD your God, and cry out to the LORD.

Then in verses 15 through 20, the situation is described again, particularly in 16-18:

Has not the food been cut off before our very eyes— joy and gladness from the house of our God? The seeds are shriveled beneath the clods. The storehouses are in ruins, the granaries have been broken down, for the grain has dried up. How the cattle moan! The herds mill about because they have no pasture; even the flocks of sheep are suffering.

That's as good a picture of the church in America as I can find. There may be milk, but very little meat. The people are hungry, the churches are in debt. The money and resources leave faster than they come in. Whatever seed is planted is wasted in the ground. Any growth we see is transfer growth as the herds mill about seeking green pasture and can find none. People will fly across the country and even move their families if they sense a real move of God. They'll latch onto any Jesus fad or manifestation that comes along because they are so desperately hungry.

Then again in chapter 2 is the same recommended solution shown:

> 12 *"Even now,"* declares the LORD, *return to me with all your heart, with fasting and weeping and mourning."* 13 *Rend your heart and not your garments. Return to the LORD your God, for he is gracious and compassionate, slow to anger and abounding in love, and he relents from sending calamity. 14 Who knows? He may turn and have pity and leave behind a blessing— grain offerings and drink offerings for the LORD your God. 15 Blow the trumpet in Zion, declare a holy fast, call a sacred assembly. 16 Gather the people, consecrate the assembly; bring together the elders, gather the children, those nursing at the breast. Let the bridegroom leave his room and the bride her chamber. 17 Let the priests, who minister before the LORD, weep between the temple porch and the altar. Let them say, "Spare your people, O LORD. Do not make your inheritance an object of scorn, a byword among the nations. Why should they say among the peoples, 'Where is their God?' "*

Then, if you do these things, the Lord shows how He will respond:

> *18 Then the LORD will be jealous for his land and take pity on his people. 19 The LORD will reply to them: "I am sending you grain, new wine and oil, enough to satisfy you fully; never again will I make you an object of scorn to the nations.*

And in the verses following, there are some other amazing promises and expressions of His mercy and loving kindness.

But it boils down to this, when then land is desolate and there is no food, when the people mill around from place to place seeking anything edible and find none, you need to:

1. Declare a Holy Fast.

2. Call a Sacred Assembly and summon the Elders.

3. Repent and weep and mourn before the altar.

Then He will turn.

So, what's a "Holy Fast"? That's in Isaiah 58. The kind of fast the Lord wants; that you break the chains, lift the yokes, free the captives, feed the hungry, clothe the naked, take in the poor wanderer, stop the malicious talk and the pointing finger and THEN He will turn and good stuff starts happening. And that doesn't just mean in the "natural" - that means free the captive spirits, feed the hungry in spirit, clothe the unarmored spirits, etc. Remember, Body, Soul and Spirit – do Isaiah 58 across all three dimensions. You take it to the Lord and have Him show you what application that might have to your own situation. These also happen to overlap with Matthew 25:31-46 (which is kind of like the final exam). Basically practice extravagant giving to the poor - the poor in spirit and the poor in money.

So, what's a "Sacred Assembly"? That would be those people who are walking in holiness and are consecrated before the Lord. The people with big cups of Jesus and no embedded red stuff. That doesn't necessarily mean the pastors. There's no guarantee they're walking in holiness just because they went to seminary. Ultimately, we're going to have to let God call the meeting because we don't know who is and who isn't consecrated at any given moment. How many need to be there? Don't know. Who are the Elders? Don't know. Just commit to Him that you want to call a sacred assembly and He'll tell you how and arrange to have all the right people there. This is VERY important to Him and He doesn't mind helping. Or He'll gather whoever is available and ask you to repent for yourself first and get cleaned out before you repent on behalf of anybody else.

I believe intercession and repentance is required to restore a divided body. Preferably lots of people, but even one will do if they are sanctified before the Lord and willing to stand in the gap for the rest of the Body. Are you willing to pray the prayer of Moses? Even that you would be blotted out of the Book if only they would be forgiven and the Body would be One again? You better have a lot of Jesus in you to pray THAT prayer!

In John 17, Jesus prayed in the Garden of Gethsemane that we would be one as He and the Father are one. God loves His Son desperately, and yet that ONE prayer has remained unanswered. Maybe because none of us are praying it in agreement with Jesus. Can there be anything more urgent or more important than the restoration of the Body of Christ? Maybe we should all hit our knees and repent for the mess we've made and start praying that one prayer with Jesus until God answers it.

OK, end of sermon. You want practical stuff? Get on the website and download the "Cup" model graphics and powerpoint presentation. Use the "Fill My Cup, Lord" article and graphics as the beginning framework. Appendix A of this document and the verses in Appendix B are great to show the scriptural justifications for this. Just show them examples of how the Holy Spirit can be poured out on another. If your whole fellowship isn't ready for it, ask the Lord to show you the ones with the most wisdom and discernment and comfort level with spiritual matters and teach them one at a time until it begins an undercurrent of acceptance.

But ultimately, just do whatever God tells you. Don't listen to me. Check everything with Him.

Pray this (or whatever He tells you to pray):

Lord, please show me my cup. Please give me wisdom and discernment and help me hear Your voice really well so that You can guide my steps in implementing this. I believe there is something to this, Lord. Please confirm it and write it on my heart. I don't want to follow ANY man, Lord. Just you and you alone are worthy and just and true. You be my head and take me where You want me to go. I love You, Lord. Whatever it takes. Amen.

APPENDIX A

You Can Be Filled With GOOD Stuff:

The Lord – Psalm 16:5; 1 Cor 10:21

Fullness of God – Eph 3:19

Spirit of God – Exod 31:3; Exod. 35:31; Eph 5:18

Glory of the Lord – Ex. 40:34-35; Num 14:21; 1 Kings 8:10-11; 2 Chron. 5:14; 2 Chron. 7:1-2; Psalm 72:19; Isa 6:3; Ezek 10:3-4; Ezek 43:5; Hag 2:7; Rev 15:8

Holy Ghost – Luke 1:15; 1:41; 1:67; 4:1; Acts 2:4; Acts 4:8; Acts 4:31, 6:3, 7:55, 9:17, 11:24, 13:9

Goodness of the Lord – Psalm 33:5

Blessing of the Lord – Deut 33:23

Fear of the Lord – Luke 5:26

All Knowledge – Rom 15:14

Knowledge of the Lord – Isaiah 11:9

Power by the spirit of the Lord and judgement – Micah 3:8

Knowledge of the glory of God – Hab 2:14

Knowledge of His will, all wisdom & understanding – Col. 1:19

Spirit of Wisdom – Exod. 28:3; 35:35; Deut. 34:9

Wisdom & understanding – I Kings 7:14

Wisdom and grace – Luke 2:40

Wisdom and beauty – Exd. 35:35; Ezek. 28:12

Judgement and righteousness – Isa. 33:5

Light – Matt. 6:22 (Luke 11:34-36)

Grace and truth – John 1:14

Faith and power – Acts 6:8

Salvation – Psalm 116:13

Righteousness – Psalm 48:10; Psalm 112:4; Matt. 5:6

Fruits of Righteousness – Phil 1:11

Comfort – 2 Cor 7:4

Consolation – Jerem. 16:7

Compassion – Psalm 78:38, 86:15, 111:4, 145:8;

Joy – John 15:11; John 16:24; Acts 2:28; 2 Tim. 1:4; I Pet 1:8; 1 John 1:4; 2 John 1:12

Joy, Peace, Hope – Rom 15:13

Mercy – Psalm 119:64

Mercy and good fruits – James 3:17
    Blessing – 1 Cor 10:16

Good – Psalm 104:28; Psalm 107:9; Ecc 6:3

Good things – Job 22:18; Luke 1:53

Good works and almsdeeds – Acts 9:36

Goodness and all knowledge – Rom 15:14

Praise and honour – Psalm 71:8

Laughter and singing/rejoicing – Psalm 126:2; Job 8:21

Precious and pleasant riches – Prov. 24:4

Horses, chariots, might men of war – Ezek. 39:20

Wonder and amazement – Acts 3:10

Trembling (to enemies) – Zech 12:2

Full of days – Job 42:17

Children/People – Psalm 127:5; Luke 14:23

Bread (Food) – Exd. 28:3; Matt 14:20; Matt 15:37; Mark 6:42; Mark 8:8; Luke 9:17; John 6:26;

Need Clean Cup: Matt 23:25; Luke 11:39; Prov. 25:4; Isaiah 66:20; 1 Thes 4:4; 2 Tim 2:21; Hebrews 9:21

Different Size Cups: Isaiah 22:24

Need Pliable Cup: Matt. 9:17 (Mar 2:22, Luke 5:37)

Need FULL Cup: Matt 25:4; Ruth 1:21

Chosen/Special Vessel:
Acts 9:15; Rom 9:21; I Thes 4:4; 2 Tim 2:20

Hated Vessels: Rom 9:22

Things that are NEVER Full:

Hell and destruction - Prov. 27:20

The Sea – Ecc. 1:7

Appetite – Ecc 6:7

Things that can be filled: Stomach, Hearts, House of the Lord/Tabernacle, People, Tribes, Nations, God, the Earth

Or You Can Be Filled With BAD Stuff:

Sin – Job 20:11; Jerem. 51:5; I Thes 2:16;

Evil and madness - Ecc 9:3

Satan, lies – Acts 5:3

Devils – 1 Corin 10:21

Confusion – Job 10:15; Acts 19:29

Heaviness – Psalm 69:20; Phil 2:26

Travail and vexation of spirit – Ecc 4:6

Tossings to and fro – Job 7:4

Drunkenness and/or nakedness – Lam. 4:21; Jerem. 12:12

Drunkenness, Sorrow, astonishment and desolation – Ez 23:33

Violence – Gen. 6:11; Gen. 6:13; Ezek 7:23, 8:17, 28:16

Violence, lies and deceit – Zeph 1:9; Micah 6:12

Lies, robbery, blood – Nahum 3:1

Abominations and filthiness – Ezra 9:11;

Abominations, filthiness of fornication – Rev. 17:4

Adultery, cannot cease from sin, beguiling, covetous practices, cursed children – 2 Peter 2:14

Bitterness – Job 9:18; Lam. 3:15

Sorrow – John 16:6

Envy, contradicting, blaspheming – Acts 13:45

Unrighteousness, fornication, wickedness, covetousness, maliciousness, full of envy, murder debate, deceit, malignity, whisperers, backbiters, haters of God, despiteful, proud, boasters, inventors of evil things, disobedient to parents, without understanding, covenant breakers, without natural affection, implacable, unmerciful – Rom 1:29-31

Wickedness – Lev. 19:29; Joel 3:13

Blood of innocents – 2 Kings 21:16; 2 Kings 24:4; Jer. 19:4

Hands full of blood – Isaiah 1:15

Bloody crimes and violence – Ezek 7:23

Blood and perverseness – Ezek. 9:9

Trouble – Job 14:1; Psalm 88:3

Heaviness – Psalm 69:20; Phil 2:26

Cursing, deceit, fraud, mischief and vanity – Psalm 10:7

Cursing and bitterness – Rom 3:14

Mischief – Prov. 12:21; Psalm 26:10

Subtilty and mischief – Acts 13:10

Deceit – Jerem 5:27

Deadly Poison – James 3:8

Extortion and excess – Matt. 23:25

Hypocrisy and iniquity – Matt. 23:28

Cruelty / Strife – Psalm 74:20; Strife – Prov. 17:1

Darkness – Matt 6:23; Luke 11:34; Rev. 16:10

No pleasure – Hosea 8:8

Their own devices/own ways – Prov 1:31; Prov 3:10; Prov 14:4

Dead men's bones and uncleanness – Matt 23:27

Carcases of detestable and abominable things – Jer 16:18

Wrath - Esther 3:5; Luke 4:28; Acts 19:28;

Wrath of God - Rev. 15:1; Rev. 15:7; Rev. 16:19

Fury of the Lord – Isa 51:17; Isa 51:20; Jer 6:11

Fury – Dan 3:19; Jer 25:15

Astonishment and desolation – Eze 23:33

Snare, fire and brimstone, tempest - Psalm 11:6

Trembling – Isa 51:17, Isa 51:22, Zech 12:2

Indignation – Esther 5:9; Isa 30:27; Jer 15:17; Acts 5:17; Rev 14:10

Judgement – Isaiah 1:21

Reproach / Shame – Lam 3:30; Hab. 2:16

Scorn and derision – Psalm 123:4; Ezek. 23:22

Contempt – Psalm 123:3

Confusion – Job 10:15

Plagues – Exd 10:6; Rev. 21:9

Madness – Jerem 51:7; Luke 6:11

Disease / Pain – Psalm 38:7; Isa 21:3

Slain – Jer 33:5; Ezek 9:7; Ezek 30:11; Ezek 32:5

APPENDIX B

Verses about Filled, Fill, Full, Fountains, Springs, Cup, Cups, Vessel, Vessels, Bowl, Bowls, Wineskins, Bottle, Bottles, Cisterns, Vats, Pot, Pots, Dwelleth (all from King James Version)

FILLED

<u>Gen 6:11</u> The earth also was corrupt before God, and the earth was **filled with violence**.

<u>Gen 6:13</u> And God said unto Noah, The end of all flesh is come before me; for the earth is **filled with violence** through them; and, behold, I will destroy them with the earth.

<u>Exd 28:3</u> And thou shalt speak unto all [that are] wise hearted, whom I have **filled with the spirit of wisdom**, that they may make Aaron's garments to consecrate him, that he may minister unto me in the priest's office.

<u>Exd 31:3</u> And I have **filled him with the spirit of God**, in wisdom, and in understanding, and in knowledge, and in all manner of workmanship,

Exd 35:31 And he hath **filled him with the spirit of God**, in wisdom, in understanding, and in knowledge, and in all manner of workmanship;

Exd 35:35 Them hath he **filled with wisdom of heart**, to work all manner of work, of the engraver, and of the cunning workman, and of the embroiderer, in blue, and in purple, in scarlet, and in fine linen, and of the weaver, [even] of them that do any work, and of those that devise cunning work.

Exd 40:34 Then a cloud covered the tent of the congregation, and the **glory of the LORD filled the tabernacle**.

Exd 40:35 And Moses was not able to enter into the tent of the congregation, because the cloud abode thereon, and the **glory of the LORD filled the tabernacle**.

Num 14:21 But [as] truly [as] I live, all the earth shall be **filled with the glory of the LORD**.

Deu 26:12 When thou hast made an end of tithing all the tithes of thine increase the third year, [which is] the year of tithing, and hast given [it] unto the Levite, the stranger, the fatherless, and the widow, that they may eat within thy gates, and **be filled**;

Deu 31:20 For when I shall have brought them into the land which I sware unto their fathers, that floweth with milk and honey; and they shall have eaten and **filled themselves**, and waxen fat; then will they turn unto other gods, and serve them, and provoke me, and break my covenant.

1Ki 7:14 He [was] a widow's son of the tribe of Naphtali, and his father [was] a man of Tyre, a worker in brass: and he was **filled with wisdom, and understanding, and cunning** to work all works in brass. And he came to king Solomon, and wrought all his work.

1Ki 8:10 And it came to pass, when the priests were come out of the holy [place], that the **cloud filled the house of the LORD**, 1Ki 8:11 So that the priests could not stand to minister because of the cloud: for the **glory of the LORD had filled** the house of the LORD.

2Ki 3:17 For thus saith the LORD, Ye shall not see wind, neither shall ye see rain; yet that valley shall be filled with water, that ye may drink, both ye, and your cattle, and your beasts.

2Ki 3:20 And it came to pass in the morning, when the meat offering was offered, that, behold, there came water by the way of Edom, and the country was filled with water.

2Ki 21:16 Moreover Manasseh shed **innocent blood** very much, till he had **filled Jerusalem** from one end to another; beside his sin wherewith he made Judah to sin, in doing [that which was] evil in the sight of the LORD.

2Ki 23:14 And he brake in pieces the images, and cut down the groves, and filled their places with the bones of men.

2Ki 24:4 And also for the innocent blood that he shed: for he **filled Jerusalem with innocent blood**; which the LORD would not pardon.

2Ch 5:13 It came even to pass, as the trumpeters and singers [were] as one, to make one sound to be heard in praising and thanking the LORD; and when they lifted up [their] voice with the trumpets and cymbals and instruments of musick, and praised the LORD, [saying], For [he is] good; for his mercy [endureth] for ever: that [then] the house was **filled with a cloud,** [even] the house of the LORD; 2Ch 5:14 So that the priests could not stand to minister by reason of the cloud: for the **glory of the LORD had filled the house of God**.

2Ch 7:1 Now when Solomon had made an end of praying, the fire came down from heaven, and consumed the burnt offering and the sacrifices; and the **glory of the LORD filled the house**. 2Ch 7:2 And the priests could not enter into the house of the LORD, because the **glory of the LORD had filled the LORD'S house**.

Ezr 9:11 Which thou hast commanded by thy servants the prophets, saying, The land, unto which ye go to possess it, is an unclean land with the filthiness of the people of the lands, with their abominations, which have **filled it from one end to another with their uncleanness**.

Neh 9:25 And they took strong cities, and a fat land, and possessed houses full of all goods, wells digged, vineyards, and oliveyards, and fruit trees in abundance: so they did eat, and **were filled, and became fat**, and delighted themselves in thy great goodness.

Job 3:15 Or with princes that had gold, who filled their houses with silver:

Job 16:8 And thou hast **filled me with wrinkles**, [which] is a witness [against me]: and my leanness rising up in me beareth witness to my face.

Job 22:18 Yet he **filled their houses with good [things]**: but the counsel of the wicked is far from me.

Psa 38:7 For my loins are **filled with a loathsome [disease]**: and [there is] no soundness in my flesh.

Psa 71:8 Let my mouth be **filled [with] thy praise [and with] thy honour all the day**.

Psa 72:19 And blessed [be] his glorious name for ever: and let the whole earth be **filled [with] his glory**; Amen, and Amen.

Psa 104:28 [That] thou givest them they gather: thou openest thine hand, they are **filled with good**.

Psa 123:3 Have mercy upon us, O LORD, have mercy upon us: for we are **exceedingly filled with contempt**.

Psa 123:4 Our soul is **exceedingly filled with the scorning** of those that are at ease, [and] with the contempt of the proud.

Psa 126:2 Then was our mouth **filled with laughter**, and our tongue with singing: then said they among the heathen, The LORD hath done great things for them.

Pro 1:31 Therefore shall they eat of the fruit of their own way, and be **filled with their own devices**.

Pro 3:10 So shall thy barns be **filled with plenty**, and thy presses shall burst out with new wine.

Pro 5:10 Lest strangers be **filled with thy wealth**; and thy labours [be] in the house of a stranger;

Pro 12:21 There shall no evil happen to the just: but the wicked shall be **filled with mischief**.

Pro 14:14 The backslider in heart shall be **filled with his own ways**: and a good man [shall be satisfied] from himself.

Pro 18:20 A man's belly shall be satisfied with the fruit of his mouth; [and] with the **increase of his lips shall he be filled**.

<u>Pro 20:17</u> Bread of deceit [is] sweet to a man; but afterwards his mouth shall be **filled with gravel.**

<u>Pro 24:4</u> And by knowledge shall the chambers be **filled with all precious and pleasant riches.**

<u>Ecc 1:8</u> All things [are] full of labour; man cannot utter [it]: the eye is not satisfied with seeing, nor the ear **filled with hearing.**

<u>Ecc 6:3</u> If a man beget an hundred [children], and live many years, so that the days of his years be many, and his soul be **not filled with good,** and also [that] he have no burial; I say, [that] an untimely birth [is] better than he.

<u>Ecc 6:7</u> All the labour of man [is] for his mouth, and yet the **appetite is not filled.**

<u>Sgs 5:2</u> I sleep, but my heart waketh: [it is] the voice of my beloved that knocketh, [saying], Open to me, my sister, my love, my dove, my undefiled: for my head is **filled with dew,** [and] my locks with the drops of the night.

<u>Isa 6:1</u> In the year that king Uzziah died I saw also the Lord sitting upon a throne, high and lifted up, and his **train filled the temple.**

<u>Isa 6:4</u> And the posts of the door moved at the voice of him that cried, and the house was **filled with smoke.**

<u>Isa 21:3</u> Therefore are my loins **filled with pain**: pangs have taken hold upon me, as the pangs of a woman that travaileth: I was bowed down at the hearing [of it]; I was dismayed at the seeing [of it].

<u>Isa 33:5</u> The LORD is exalted; for he dwelleth on high: he hath **filled Zion with judgment and righteousness.**

<u>Isa 34:6</u> The sword of the LORD is **filled with blood**, it is made fat with fatness, [and] with the blood of lambs and goats, with the fat of the kidneys of rams: for the LORD hath a sacrifice in Bozrah, and a great slaughter in the land of Idumea.

<u>Isa 43:24</u> Thou hast bought me no sweet cane with money, neither hast thou **filled me with the fat of thy sacrifices**: but thou hast made me to serve with thy sins, thou hast wearied me with thine iniquities.

<u>Isa 65:20</u> There shall be no more thence an infant of days, nor an old man that hath not **filled his days**: for the child shall die an hundred

years old; but the sinner [being] an hundred years old shall be accursed.

Jer 13:12 Therefore thou shalt speak unto them this word; Thus saith the LORD God of Israel, Every bottle shall be **filled with wine**: and they shall say unto thee, Do we not certainly know that every bottle shall be filled with wine?

Jer 15:17 I sat not in the assembly of the mockers, nor rejoiced; I sat alone because of thy hand: for thou hast **filled me with indignation**.

Jer 16:18 And first I will recompense their iniquity and their sin double; because they have defiled my land, they have **filled mine inheritance with the carcases of their detestable and abominable things**.

Jer 19:4 Because they have forsaken me, and have estranged this place, and have burned incense in it unto other gods, whom neither they nor their fathers have known, nor the kings of Judah, and have **filled this place with the blood of innocents**;

Jer 46:12 The nations have heard of thy shame, and thy **cry hath filled the land**: for the mighty man hath stumbled against the mighty, [and] they are fallen both together.

Jer 51:5 For Israel [hath] not [been] forsaken, nor Judah of his God, of the LORD of hosts; though their land was **filled with sin against the Holy One of Israel**.

Jer 51:34 Nebuchadrezzar the king of Babylon hath devoured me, he hath crushed me, he hath made me an empty vessel, he hath **swallowed me up like a dragon**, he hath **filled his belly with my delicates**, he hath cast me out.

Lam 3:15 He hath **filled me with bitterness**, he hath made me drunken with wormwood.

Lam 3:30 He giveth [his] cheek to him that smiteth him: he is **filled full with reproac**h.

Eze 8:17 Then he said unto me, Hast thou seen [this], O son of man? Is it a light thing to the house of Judah that they commit the abominations which they commit here? for they have **filled the land with violence**, and have returned to provoke me to anger: and, lo, they put the branch to their nose.

Eze 10:3 Now the cherubims stood on the right side of the house, when the man went in; and the cloud **filled the inner court**. Eze 10:4 Then the glory of the LORD went up from the cherub, [and stood] over the threshold of the house; and the house was filled with the cloud, and the court was **full of the brightness of the LORD'S glory**.

Eze 11:6 Ye have multiplied your slain in this city, and ye have **filled the streets thereof with the slain**.

Eze 23:33 Thou shalt be **filled with drunkenness and sorrow**, with the cup of astonishment and desolation, with the cup of thy sister Samaria.

Eze 28:16 By the multitude of thy merchandise they have **filled the midst of thee with violence**, and thou hast sinned: therefore I will cast thee as profane out of the mountain of God: and I will destroy thee, O covering cherub, from the midst of the stones of fire.

Eze 36:38 As the holy flock, as the flock of Jerusalem in her solemn feasts; so shall the waste cities be **filled with flocks of men**: and they shall know that I [am] the LORD.

Eze 39:20 Thus ye shall be filled at my table with horses and chariots, with mighty men, and with all men of war, saith the Lord GOD.

Eze 43:5 So the spirit took me up, and brought me into the inner court; and, behold, the **glory of the LORD filled the house**.

Eze 44:4 Then brought he me the way of the north gate before the house: and I looked, and, behold, the **glory of the LORD filled the house of the LORD**: and I fell upon my face.

Dan 2:35 Then was the iron, the clay, the brass, the silver, and the gold, broken to pieces together, and became like the chaff of the summer threshingfloors; and the wind carried them away, that no place was found for them: and the stone that smote the image became a great mountain, and **filled the whole earth**.

Hsa 13:6 According to their pasture, so were they filled; they were filled, and their heart was exalted; therefore have they forgotten me.

Hab 2:14 For the earth shall be **filled with the knowledge of the glory of the LORD**, as the waters cover the sea.

Hab 2:16 Thou art **filled with shame** for glory: drink thou also, and let thy foreskin be uncovered: the cup of the LORD'S right hand shall be turned unto thee, and shameful spewing [shall be] on thy glory.

Hag 1:6 Ye have sown much, and bring in little; ye eat, but ye have not enough; ye drink, but ye are **not filled** with drink; ye clothe you, but there is none warm; and he that earneth wages earneth wages [to put it] into a bag with holes.

Zec 9:13 When I have bent Judah for me, **filled the bow** with Ephraim, and raised up thy sons, O Zion, against thy sons, O Greece, and made thee as the sword of a mighty man.

Zec 9:15 The LORD of hosts shall defend them; and they shall devour, and subdue with sling stones; and they shall drink, [and] make a noise as through wine; and they shall be **filled like bowls, [and] as the corners of the altar.**

Mat 5:6 Blessed [are] they which do **hunger and thirst after righteousness: for they shall be filled**.

Mat 14:20 And they did all eat, and were filled: and they took up of the fragments that remained twelve baskets full.

Mat 15:37 And they did all eat, and were filled: and they took up of the broken [meat] that was left seven baskets full.

Mar 2:21 No man also seweth a piece of new cloth on an old garment: else the new piece that filled it up taketh away from the old, and the rent is made worse.

Mar 6:42 And they did all eat, and were filled.

Mar 7:27 But Jesus said unto her, **Let the children first be filled**: for it is not meet to take the children's bread, and to cast [it] unto the dogs.

Mar 8:8 So they did eat, and were filled: and they took up of the broken [meat] that was left seven baskets.

Luk 1:15 For he shall be great in the sight of the Lord, and shall drink neither wine nor strong drink; and he shall be **filled with the Holy Ghost**, even from his mother's womb.

Luk 1:41 And it came to pass, that, when Elisabeth heard the salutation of Mary, the babe leaped in her womb; and Elisabeth was **filled with the Holy Ghost**:

Luk 1:53 He hath **filled the hungry with good things**; and the rich he hath sent empty away.

Luk 1:67 And his father Zacharias was **filled with the Holy Ghost**, and prophesied, saying,

Luk 2:40 And the child grew, and waxed strong in spirit, **filled with wisdom: and the grace of God** was upon him.

Luk 3:5 Every valley shall be filled, and every mountain and hill shall be brought low; and the crooked shall be made straight, and the rough ways [shall be] made smooth;

Luk 4:28 And all they in the synagogue, when they heard these things, were **filled with wrath**,

Luk 5:26 And they were all amazed, and they glorified God, and were **filled with fear**, saying, We have seen strange things to day.

Luk 6:11 And they were **filled with madness**; and communed one with another what they might do to Jesus.

Luk 6:21 Blessed [are ye] that hunger now: for **ye shall be filled.** Blessed [are ye] that weep now: for ye shall laugh.

Luk 8:23 But as they sailed he fell asleep: and there came down a storm of wind on the lake; and they were filled [with water], and were in jeopardy.

Luk 9:17 And they did eat, and were **all filled**: and there was taken up of fragments that remained to them twelve baskets.

Luk 14:23 And the lord said unto the servant, Go out into the highways and hedges, and compel [them] to come in, that my **house may be filled**.

Luk 15:16 And he would fain have filled his belly with the husks that the swine did eat: and no man gave unto him.

Jhn 2:7 Jesus saith unto them, Fill the waterpots with water. And they filled them up to the brim.

Jhn 6:12 When they were filled, he said unto his disciples, Gather up the fragments that remain, that nothing be lost.

Jhn 6:13 Therefore they gathered [them] together, and filled twelve baskets with the fragments of the five barley loaves, which remained over and above unto them that had eaten.

Jhn 6:26 Jesus answered them and said, Verily, verily, I say unto you, Ye seek me, not because ye saw the miracles, but because ye did eat of the loaves, and were filled.

Jhn 12:3 Then took Mary a pound of ointment of spikenard, very costly, and anointed the feet of Jesus, and wiped his feet with her hair: and the house was filled with the odour of the ointment.

Jhn 16:6 But because I have said these things unto you, **sorrow hath filled your heart**.

Jhn 19:29 Now there was set a vessel full of vinegar: and they filled a spunge with vinegar, and put [it] upon hyssop, and put [it] to his mouth.

Act 2:2 And suddenly there came a sound from heaven as of a rushing mighty wind, and it **filled all the house** where they were sitting.

Act 2:4 And they were all **filled with the Holy Ghost**, and began to speak with other tongues, as the Spirit gave them utterance.

Act 3:10 And they knew that it was he which sat for alms at the Beautiful gate of the temple: and they were **filled with wonder and amazement** at that which had happened unto him.

Act 4:8 Then Peter, **filled with the Holy Ghost**, said unto them, Ye rulers of the people, and elders of Israel,

Act 4:31 And when they had prayed, the place was shaken where they were assembled together; and they were **all filled with the Holy Ghost**, and they spake the word of God with boldness.

Act 5:3 But Peter said, Ananias, why hath **Satan filled thine heart** to lie to the Holy Ghost, and to keep back [part] of the price of the land?

Act 5:17 Then the high priest rose up, and all they that were with him, (which is the sect of the Sadducees,) and were **filled with indignation**,

Act 5:28 Saying, Did not we straitly command you that ye should not teach in this name? and, behold, ye have filled Jerusalem with your doctrine, and intend to bring this man's blood upon us.

Act 9:17 And Ananias went his way, and entered into the house; and putting his hands on him said, Brother Saul, the Lord, [even] Jesus, that appeared unto thee in the way as thou camest, hath sent me, that thou mightest receive thy sight, and be **filled with the Holy Ghost**.

Act 13:9 Then Saul, (who also [is called] Paul,) **filled with the Holy Ghost**, set his eyes on him,

Act 13:45 But when the Jews saw the multitudes, they were **filled with envy**, and spake against those things which were spoken by Paul, contradicting and blaspheming.

Act 13:52 And the disciples were **filled with joy, and with the Holy Ghost.**

Act 19:29 And the whole city was **filled with confusion**: and having caught Gaius and Aristarchus, men of Macedonia, Paul's companions in travel, they rushed with one accord into the theatre.

Rom 1:29 Being **filled with all unrighteousness, fornication, wickedness, covetousness, maliciousness; full of envy, murder, debate, deceit, malignity; whisperers,**

Rom 15:14 And I myself also am persuaded of you, my brethren, that ye also are **full of goodness, filled with all knowledge**, able also to admonish one another.

Rom 15:24 Whensoever I take my journey into Spain, I will come to you: for I trust to see you in my journey, and to be brought on my way thitherward by you, if first I be somewhat filled with your [company].

2Cr 7:4 Great [is] my boldness of speech toward you, great [is] my glorying of you: I am **filled with comfort,** I am exceeding joyful in all our tribulation.

Eph 3:19 And to know the love of Christ, which passeth knowledge, that ye might be **filled with all the fulness of God**.

Eph 5:18 And be not drunk with wine, wherein is excess; but be **filled with the Spirit;**

Phl 1:11 Being **filled with the fruits of righteousness**, which are by Jesus Christ, unto the glory and praise of God.

Col 1:9 For this cause we also, since the day we heard [it], do not cease to pray for you, and to desire that ye might be **filled with the knowledge of his will in all wisdom and spiritual understanding;**

2Ti 1:4 Greatly desiring to see thee, being mindful of thy tears, that I may be **filled with joy**;

Rev 8:5 And the angel took the censer, and **filled it with fire of the altar**, and cast [it] into the earth: and there were voices, and thunderings, and lightnings, and an earthquake.

Rev 15:1 And I saw another sign in heaven, great and marvellous, seven angels having the seven last plagues; for in them is **filled up the wrath of G**od.

Rev 15:8 And the temple was **filled with smoke from the glory of God, and from his power**; and no man was able to enter into the temple, till the seven plagues of the seven angels were fulfilled.

Rev 18:6 Reward her even as she rewarded you, and double unto her double according to her works: in the cup which she hath filled **fill to her double**.

Rev 19:21 And the remnant were slain with the sword of him that sat upon the horse, which [sword] proceeded out of his mouth: and all the fowls were **filled with their flesh**.

FILL

Lev 25:19 And the land shall yield her fruit, and ye shall eat your fill, and dwell therein in safety.

Job 8:21 Till he **fill thy mouth with laughing, and thy lips with rejoicing.**

Job 15:2 Should a wise man utter vain knowledge, and **fill his belly with the east wind**?

Job 23:4 I would order [my] cause before him, and **fill my mouth with arguments**.

Job 38:39 Wilt thou hunt the prey for the lion? or **fill the appetite of the young lions**,

Job 41:7 Canst thou **fill his skin with barbed irons**? or his head with fish spears?

Psa 81:10 I [am] the LORD thy God, which brought thee out of the land of Egypt: open thy mouth wide, and **I will fill it**.

Psa 83:16 **Fill their faces with shame**; that they may seek thy name, O LORD.

Psa 110:6 He shall judge among the heathen, he shall **fill [the places] with the dead bodies**; he shall wound the heads over many countries.

Pro 1:13 We shall find all precious substance, we shall **fill our houses with spoil**:

Pro 7:18 Come, let us take our **fill of love** until the morning: let us solace ourselves with loves.

Pro 8:21 That I may cause those that love me to inherit substance; and I will **fill their treasures**.

Isa 27:6 He shall cause them that come of Jacob to take root: Israel shall blossom and bud, and fill the face of the world with fruit.

Isa 56:12 Come ye, [say they], I will fetch wine, and we will **fill ourselves with strong drink**; and to morrow shall be as this day, [and] much more abundant.

Jer 13:13 Then shalt thou say unto them, Thus saith the LORD, Behold, I will **fill all** the inhabitants of this land, even the kings that sit upon David's throne, and the priests, and the prophets, and all the inhabitants of Jerusalem, **with drunkenness.**

Jer 23:24 Can any hide himself in secret places that I shall not see him? saith the LORD. Do not I fill heaven and earth? saith the LORD.

Jer 33:5 They come to fight with the Chaldeans, but [it is] to **fill them with the dead bodies of men**, whom I have slain in mine anger and in my fury, and for all whose wickedness I have hid my face from this city.

Eze 3:3 And he said unto me, Son of man, cause thy belly to eat, and fill thy bowels with this roll that I give thee. Then did I eat [it]; and it was in my mouth as honey for sweetness.

Eze 7:19 They shall cast their silver in the streets, and their gold shall be removed: their silver and their gold shall not be able to deliver them in the day of the wrath of the LORD: they shall not satisfy their souls, neither fill their bowels: because it is the stumblingblock of their iniquity.

Eze 9:7 And he said unto them, Defile the house, and **fill the courts with the slain**: go ye forth. And they went forth, and slew in the city.

Eze 10:2 And he spake unto the man clothed with linen, and said, Go in between the wheels, [even] under the cherub, and **fill thine hand with coals of fire** from between the cherubims, and scatter [them] over the city. And he went in in my sight.

Eze 30:11 He and his people with him, the terrible of the nations, shall be brought to destroy the land: and they shall draw their swords against Egypt, and **fill the land with the slain.**

Eze 32:4 Then will I leave thee upon the land, I will cast thee forth upon the open field, and will cause all the fowls of the heaven to remain upon thee, and I will fill the beasts of the whole earth with thee.

Zep 1:9 In the same day also will I punish all those that leap on the threshold, which **fill their masters' houses with violence and deceit.**

Hag 2:7 And I will shake all nations, and the desire of all nations shall come: and I will **fill this house with glory**, saith the LORD of hosts.

Mat 9:16 No man putteth a piece of new cloth unto an old garment, for that which is put in to fill it up taketh from the garment, and the rent is made worse.

Mat 15:33 And his disciples say unto him, Whence should we have so much bread in the wilderness, as to fill so great a multitude?

Mat 23:32 Fill ye up then the measure of your fathers.

Jhn 2:7 Jesus saith unto them, Fill the waterpots with water. And they filled them up to the brim.

Rom 15:13 Now the God of hope **fill you with all joy and peace in believing**, that ye may abound in hope, through the power of the Holy Ghost.

Eph 4:10 He that descended is the same also that ascended up far above all heavens, that he might **fill all things.)**

Col 1:24 Who now rejoice in my sufferings for you, and fill up that which is behind of the afflictions of Christ in my flesh for his body's sake, which is the church:

1Th 2:16 Forbidding us to speak to the Gentiles that they might be saved, to fill up their sins alway: for the wrath is come upon them to the uttermost.

Rev 18:6 Reward her even as she rewarded you, and double unto her double according to her works: in the cup which she hath filled **fill to her double**.

FILLETH

Job 9:18 He will not suffer me to take my breath, but **filleth me with bitterness**.

Psa 107:9 For he satisfieth the longing soul, and **filleth the hungry soul with goodness**.

Psa 147:14 He maketh peace [in] thy borders, [and] filleth thee with the finest of the wheat.

Eph 1:23 Which is his body, the fulness of him that filleth all in all.

FULL

Lev 19:29 Do not prostitute thy daughter, to cause her to be a whore; lest the land fall to whoredom, and the land become **full of wickedness**.

Deu 33:23 And of Naphtali he said, O Naphtali, satisfied with favour, and full with the blessing of the LORD: possess thou the west and the south.

Deu 34:9 And Joshua the son of Nun was **full of the spirit of wisdom**; for Moses had laid his hands upon him: and the children of Israel hearkened unto him, and did as the LORD commanded Moses.

2Ki 4:4 And when thou art come in, thou shalt shut the door upon thee and upon thy sons, and shalt pour out into all those vessels, and thou shalt set aside that which is full.

2Ki 4:6 And it came to pass, when the vessels were full, that she said unto her son, Bring me yet a vessel. And he said unto her, [There is] not a vessel more. And the oil stayed.

Est 3:5 And when Haman saw that Mordecai bowed not, nor did him reverence, then was Haman **full of wrath**.

Est 5:9 Then went Haman forth that day joyful and with a glad heart: but when Haman saw Mordecai in the king's gate, that he stood not up, nor moved for him, he was **full of indignation** against Mordecai.

Job 7:4 When I lie down, I say, When shall I arise, and the night be gone? and I am **full of tossings to and fro unto the dawning of the day**.

Job 10:15 If I be wicked, woe unto me; and [if] I be righteous, [yet] will I not lift up my head. [I am] **full of confusion**; therefore see thou mine affliction;

Job 14:1 Man [that is] born of a woman [is] of few days, and **full of trouble**.

Job 20:11 His bones are **full [of the sin] of his youth**, which shall lie down with him in the dust.

Job 21:24 His breasts are **full of milk**, and his bones are moistened with marrow.

Job 42:17 So Job died, [being] old and **full of days**.

Psa 10:7 His mouth is **full of cursing and deceit and fraud**: under his tongue [is] mischief and vanity.

Psa 26:10 In whose hands [is] mischief, and their right hand is **full of bribes**.

Psa 29:4 The voice of the LORD [is] powerful; the voice of the LORD [is] **full of majesty**.

Psa 33:5 He loveth righteousness and judgment: the earth is **full of the goodness of the LORD**.

Psa 48:10 According to thy name, O God, so [is] thy praise unto the ends of the earth: thy right hand is **full of righteousness.**

Psa 69:20 Reproach hath broken my heart; and I am **full of heaviness**: and I looked [for some] to take pity, but [there was] none; and for comforters, but I found none.

Psa 73:10 Therefore his people return hither: and **waters of a full [cup] are wrung out to them**.

Psa 74:20 Have respect unto the covenant: for the dark places of the earth are **full of the habitations of cruelty**.

Psa 75:8 For in the hand of the LORD [there is] a cup, and the wine is red; it is full of mixture; and he poureth out of the same: but the dregs thereof, all the wicked of the earth shall wring [them] out, [and] drink [them].

Psa 78:38 But he, [being] **full of compassion**, forgave [their] iniquity, and destroyed [them] not: yea, many a time turned he his anger away, and did not stir up all his wrath.

Psa 86:15 But thou, O Lord, [art] a God **full of compassion**, and gracious, longsuffering, and plenteous in mercy and truth.

Psa 88:3 For my soul is **full of troubles**: and my life draweth nigh unto the grave.

Psa 104:24 O LORD, how manifold are thy works! in wisdom hast thou made them all: the earth is **full of thy riches**.

Psa 111:4 He hath made his wonderful works to be remembered: the LORD [is] gracious and **full of compassion**.

Psa 112:4 Unto the upright there ariseth light in the darkness: [he is] gracious, and **full of compassion, and righteous**.

Psa 119:64 The earth, O LORD, is **full of thy mercy**: teach me thy statutes.

Psa 127:5 Happy [is] the man that hath his quiver full of them: they shall not be ashamed, but they shall speak with the enemies in the gate.

Psa 145:8 The LORD [is] gracious, and **full of compassion**; slow to anger, and of great mercy.

Pro 17:1 Better [is] a dry morsel, and quietness therewith, than an house **full of sacrifices [with] strife**.

Pro 27:7 The full soul loatheth an honeycomb; but to the hungry soul every bitter thing is sweet.

Pro 27:20 **Hell and destruction are never full**; so the eyes of man are never satisfied.

Pro 30:9 Lest I be full, and deny [thee], and say, Who [is] the LORD? or lest I be poor, and steal, and take the name of my God [in vain].

Ecc 1:7 All the rivers run into the sea; yet the sea [is] not full; unto the place from whence the rivers come, thither they return again.

Ecc 1:8 All things [are] **full of labour**; man cannot utter [it]: the eye is not satisfied with seeing, nor the ear filled with hearing.

Ecc 4:6 Better [is] an handful [with] quietness, than both the hands **full [with] travail and vexation of spirit.**

Ecc 9:3 This [is] an evil among all [things] that are done under the sun, that [there is] one event unto all: yea, also the heart of the sons of men is **full of evil**, and madness [is] in their heart while they live, and after that [they go] to the dead.

Ecc 10:14 A fool also is **full of words**: a man cannot tell what shall be; and what shall be after him, who can tell him?

Isa 1:11 To what purpose [is] the multitude of your sacrifices unto me? saith the LORD: I am **full of the burnt offerings of rams**, and the fat of fed beasts; and I delight not in the blood of bullocks, or of lambs, or of he goats.

Isa 1:15 And when ye spread forth your hands, I will hide mine eyes from you: yea, when ye make many prayers, I will not hear: your hands are **full of blood**.

Isa 1:21 How is the faithful city become an harlot! it was **full of judgment**; righteousness lodged in it; but now murderers.

Isa 2:7 Their land also is **full of silver and gold**, neither [is there any] end of their treasures; their land is also **full of horses**, neither [is there any] end of their chariots: Isa 2:8 Their land also is **full of idols**; they worship the work of their own hands, that which their own fingers have made:

Isa 6:3 And one cried unto another, and said, Holy, holy, holy, [is] the LORD of hosts: the whole earth [is] **full of his glory**.

Isa 11:9 They shall not hurt nor destroy in all my holy mountain: for the earth shall be **full of the knowledge of the LORD**, as the waters cover the sea.

Isa 30:27 Behold, the name of the LORD cometh from far, burning [with] his anger, and the burden [thereof is] heavy: his lips are **full of indignation**, and his tongue as a devouring fire:

Isa 51:20 Thy sons have fainted, they lie at the head of all the streets, as a wild bull in a net: they are **full of the fury of the LORD**, the rebuke of thy God.

Jer 5:27 As a cage is full of birds, so [are] their houses **full of deceit**: therefore they are become great, and waxen rich.

<u>Jer 6:11</u> Therefore I am **full of the fury of the LORD**; I am weary with holding in: **I will pour it out** upon the children abroad, and upon the assembly of young men together: for even the husband with the wife shall be taken, the aged with [him that is] **full of days**.

<u>Jer 23:10</u> For the land is **full of adulterers**; for because of swearing the land mourneth; the pleasant places of the wilderness are dried up, and their course is evil, and their force [is] not right.

<u>Lam 3:30</u> He giveth [his] cheek to him that smiteth him: he is **filled full with reproach**.

<u>Eze 7:23</u> Make a chain: for the land is **full of bloody crimes**, and the city is full of violence.

<u>Eze 9:9</u> Then said he unto me, The iniquity of the house of Israel and Judah [is] exceeding great, and the land is **full of blood**, and the city **full of perverseness**: for they say, The LORD hath forsaken the earth, and the LORD seeth not.

<u>Eze 28:12</u> Son of man, take up a lamentation upon the king of Tyrus, and say unto him, Thus saith the Lord GOD; Thou sealest up the sum, **full of wisdom**, and perfect in beauty.

<u>Dan 3:19</u> Then was Nebuchadnezzar **full of fury**, and the form of his visage was changed against Shadrach, Meshach, and Abednego: [therefore] he spake, and commanded that they should heat the furnace one seven times more than it was wont to be heated.

<u>Joe 3:13</u> Put ye in the sickle, for the harvest is ripe: come, get you down; for the press is **full, the fats overflow; for their wickedness [is] great**.

<u>Mic 3:8</u> But truly I am **full of power by the spirit of the LORD, and of judgment, and of might,** to declare unto Jacob his transgression, and to Israel his sin.

<u>Mic 6:12</u> For the rich men thereof are **full of violence**, and the inhabitants thereof have spoken lies, and their tongue [is] deceitful in their mouth.

<u>Nah 3:1</u> Woe to the bloody city! it [is] all **full of lies** [and] robbery; the prey departeth not;

Hab 3:3 God came from Teman, and the Holy One from mount Paran. Selah. His glory covered the heavens, and the earth was **full of his praise.**

Mat 6:22 The light of the body is the eye: if therefore thine eye be single, thy whole body shall be **full of light.** Mat 6:23 But if thine eye be evil, thy whole body shall be **full of darkness**. If therefore the light that is in thee be darkness, how great [is] that darkness!

Mat 23:25 Woe unto you, scribes and Pharisees, hypocrites! for ye make clean the outside of the cup and of the platter, but within they are **full of extortion and excess**.

Mat 23:27 Woe unto you, scribes and Pharisees, hypocrites! for ye are like unto whited sepulchres, which indeed appear beautiful outward, but are within **full of dead [men's] bones, and of all uncleanness.**

Mat 23:28 Even so ye also outwardly appear righteous unto men, but within ye are **full of hypocrisy and iniquity**.

Luk 4:1 And Jesus being **full of the Holy Ghost** returned from Jordan, and was led by the Spirit into the wilderness,

Luk 6:25 Woe unto you that are full! for ye shall hunger. Woe unto you that laugh now! for ye shall mourn and weep.

Luk 11:34 The light of the body is the eye: therefore when thine eye is single, thy whole body also is **full of light**; but when [thine eye] is evil, thy body also [is] **full of darkness**.

Luk 11:36 If thy whole body therefore [be] **full of light**, having no part dark, the whole shall be **full of light**, as when the bright shining of a candle doth give thee light.

Luk 11:39 And the Lord said unto him, Now do ye Pharisees make clean the outside of the cup and the platter; but your inward part is **full of ravening and wickedness**.

Jhn 1:14 And the Word was made flesh, and dwelt among us, (and we beheld his glory, the glory as of the only begotten of the Father,) **full of grace and truth**.

Jhn 15:11 These things have I spoken unto you, that my joy might remain in you, and [that] your **joy might be full**.

Jhn 16:24 Hitherto have ye asked nothing in my name: ask, and ye shall receive, that your **joy may be full**.

Act 2:28 Thou hast made known to me the ways of life; thou shalt make me **full of joy** with thy countenance.

Act 6:3 Wherefore, brethren, look ye out among you seven men of honest report, **full of the Holy Ghost and wisdom**, whom we may appoint over this business.

Act 6:5 And the saying pleased the whole multitude: and they chose Stephen, a man **full of faith and of the Holy Ghost**, and Philip, and Prochorus, and Nicanor, and Timon, and Parmenas, and Nicolas a proselyte of Antioch:

Act 6:8 And Stephen, **full of faith and power**, did great wonders and miracles among the people.

Act 7:55 But he, being **full of the Holy Ghost**, looked up stedfastly into heaven, and saw the glory of God, and Jesus standing on the right hand of God,

Act 9:36 Now there was at Joppa a certain disciple named Tabitha, which by interpretation is called Dorcas: this woman was **full of good works and almsdeeds** which she did.

Act 11:24 For he was a good man, and **full of the Holy Ghost and of faith**: and much people was added unto the Lord.

Act 13:10 And said, O **full of all subtilty and all mischief**, [thou] child of the devil, [thou] enemy of all righteousness, wilt thou not cease to pervert the right ways of the Lord?

Act 19:28 And when they heard [these sayings], they were **full of wrath**, and cried out, saying, Great [is] Diana of the Ephesians.

Rom 1:29 Being **filled with all unrighteousness, fornication, wickedness, covetousness, maliciousness; full of envy, murder, debate, deceit, malignity; whisperers,**

Rom 3:14 Whose mouth [is] **full of cursing and bitterness**:

Rom 15:14 And I myself also am persuaded of you, my brethren, that ye also are **full of goodness**, filled with all knowledge, able also to admonish one another.

Phl 2:26 For he longed after you all, and was **full of heaviness**, because that ye had heard that he had been sick.

Jam 3:8 But the tongue can no man tame; [it is] an unruly evil, **full of deadly poison.**

Jam 3:17 But the wisdom that is from above is first pure, then peaceable, gentle, [and] easy to be intreated, **full of mercy** and good fruits, without partiality, and without hypocrisy.

1Pe 1:8 Whom having not seen, ye love; in whom, though now ye see [him] not, yet believing, ye rejoice with joy unspeakable and **full of glory**:

2Pe 2:14 Having eyes **full of adultery**, and that cannot cease from sin; beguiling unstable souls: an heart they have exercised with covetous practices; cursed children:

1Jo 1:4 And these things write we unto you, that your **joy may be full**.

2Jo 1:12 Having many things to write unto you, I would not [write] with paper and ink: but I trust to come unto you, and speak face to face, that our **joy may be full.**

Rev 15:7 And one of the four beasts gave unto the seven angels seven golden vials **full of the wrath of God**, who liveth for ever and ever.

Rev 16:10 And the fifth angel poured out his vial upon the seat of the beast; and his kingdom was **full of darkness**; and they gnawed their tongues for pain,

Rev 17:3 So he carried me away in the spirit into the wilderness: and I saw a woman sit upon a scarlet coloured beast, **full of names of blasphemy**, having seven heads and ten horns.

Rev 17:4 And the woman was arrayed in purple and scarlet colour, and decked with gold and precious stones and pearls, having a golden cup in her hand **full of abominations and filthiness of her fornication:**

Rev 21:9 And there came unto me one of the seven angels which had the seven vials **full of the seven last plagues**, and talked with me, saying, Come hither, I will shew thee the bride, the Lamb's wife.

FOUNTAIN / SPRING / WELL

<u>Lev 11:36</u> Nevertheless a fountain or pit, [wherein there is] plenty of water, shall be clean: but that which toucheth their carcase shall be unclean.

<u>Lev 20:18</u> And if a man shall lie with a woman having her sickness, and shall uncover her nakedness; he hath discovered her fountain, and she hath uncovered the fountain of her blood: and both of them shall be cut off from among their people.

<u>Deu 33:28</u> Israel then shall dwell in safety alone: the fountain of Jacob [shall be] upon a land of corn and wine; also his heavens shall drop down dew.

<u>Psa 36:9</u> For with thee [is] the **fountain of life**: in thy light shall we see light.

<u>Psa 68:26</u> Bless ye God in the congregations, [even] the Lord, from the **fountain of Israel**.

<u>Psa 74:15</u> Thou didst cleave the fountain and the flood: thou driedst up mighty rivers.

<u>Psa 114:8</u> Which turned the rock [into] a standing water, the flint into a fountain of waters.

<u>Pro 5:18</u> Let thy fountain be blessed: and rejoice with the wife of thy youth.

<u>Pro 13:14</u> The law of the wise [is] a **fountain of life**, to depart from the snares of death.

<u>Pro 14:27</u> The fear of the LORD [is] a **fountain of life**, to depart from the snares of death.

<u>Pro 25:26</u> A righteous man falling down before the wicked [is as] a **troubled fountain, and a corrupt spring.**

<u>Ecc 12:6</u> Or ever the silver cord be loosed, or the golden bowl be broken, or the pitcher be broken at the fountain, or the wheel broken at the cistern.

<u>Sgs 4:12</u> A garden inclosed [is] my sister, [my] spouse; a spring shut up, a **fountain sealed**.

<u>Sgs 4:15</u> A fountain of gardens, a well of **living waters**, and streams from Lebanon.

Jer 2:13 For my people have committed two evils; they have forsaken me the **fountain of living waters**, [and] hewed them out cisterns, broken cisterns, that can hold no water.

Jer 6:7 As a fountain casteth out her waters, so she casteth out her wickedness: violence and spoil is heard in her; before me continually [is] grief and wounds.

Jer 9:1 Oh that my head were waters, and mine eyes a **fountain of tears**, that I might weep day and night for the slain of the daughter of my people!

Jer 17:13 O LORD, the hope of Israel, all that forsake thee shall be ashamed, [and] they that depart from me shall be written in the earth, because they have forsaken the LORD, the **fountain of living waters**.

Hsa 13:15 Though he be fruitful among [his] brethren, an east wind shall come, the wind of the LORD shall come up from the wilderness, and his spring shall become dry, and his **fountain shall be dried up**: he shall spoil the treasure of all pleasant vessels.

Joe 3:18 And it shall come to pass in that day, [that] the mountains shall drop down new wine, and the hills shall flow with milk, and all the rivers of Judah shall flow with waters, and a fountain shall come forth of the house of the LORD, and shall water the valley of Shittim.

Zec 13:1 In that day there shall be a fountain opened to the house of David and to the inhabitants of Jerusalem for sin and for uncleanness.

Mar 5:29 And straightway the fountain of her blood was dried up; and she felt in [her] body that she was healed of that plague.

Jam 3:11 Doth a fountain send forth at the same place sweet [water] and bitter?

Jam 3:12 Can the fig tree, my brethren, bear olive berries? either a vine, figs? so [can] no fountain both yield salt water and fresh.

Rev 21:6 And he said unto me, It is done. I am Alpha and Omega, the beginning and the end. **I will give unto him that is athirst of the fountain of the water of life freely.**

FOUNTAINS / SPRINGS / WELLS

<u>Gen 7:11</u> In the six hundredth year of Noah's life, in the second month, the seventeenth day of the month, the same day were all the fountains of the great deep broken up, and the windows of heaven were opened.

<u>Gen 8:2</u> The fountains also of the deep and the windows of heaven were stopped, and the rain from heaven was restrained;

<u>Deu 8:7</u> For the LORD thy God bringeth thee into a good land, a land of brooks of water, of fountains and depths that spring out of valleys and hills;

<u>1Ki 18:5</u> And Ahab said unto Obadiah, Go into the land, unto all fountains of water, and unto all brooks: peradventure we may find grass to save the horses and mules alive, that we lose not all the beasts.

<u>2Ch 32:3</u> He took counsel with his princes and his mighty men to stop the waters of the fountains which [were] without the city: and they did help him.

<u>2Ch 32:4</u> So there was gathered much people together, who stopped all the fountains, and the brook that ran through the midst of the land, saying, Why should the kings of Assyria come, and find much water?

<u>Pro 5:16</u> Let thy fountains be dispersed abroad, [and] rivers of waters in the streets.

<u>Pro 8:24</u> When [there were] no depths, I was brought forth; when [there were] no fountains abounding with water.

<u>Pro 8:28</u> When he established the clouds above: when he strengthened the fountains of the deep:

<u>Isa 41:18</u> I will open rivers in high places, and fountains in the midst of the valleys: I will make the wilderness a pool of water, and the dry land springs of water.

<u>Rev 7:17</u> For the Lamb which is in the midst of the throne shall feed them, and shall lead them unto **living fountains of waters**: and God shall wipe away all tears from their eyes.

Rev 8:10 And the third angel sounded, and there fell a great star from heaven, burning as it were a lamp, and it fell upon the third part of the rivers, and upon the fountains of waters;

Rev 14:7 Saying with a loud voice, Fear God, and give glory to him; for the hour of his judgment is come: and worship him that made heaven, and earth, and the sea, and the fountains of waters.

Rev 16:4 And the third angel poured out his vial upon the rivers and fountains of waters; and they became blood.

CUP

Psa 11:6 Upon the wicked he shall rain snares, fire and brimstone, and an horrible tempest: [this shall be] the **portion of their cup**.

Psa 16:5 The LORD [is] the portion of mine inheritance and of my cup: thou maintainest my lot.

Psa 23:5 Thou preparest a table before me in the presence of mine enemies: thou anointest my head with oil; **my cup runneth over**.

Psa 73:10 Therefore his people return hither: and waters of a full [cup] are wrung out to them.

Psa 75:8 For in the hand of the LORD [there is] a cup, and the wine is red; it is full of mixture; and he poureth out of the same: but the dregs thereof, all the wicked of the earth shall wring [them] out, [and] drink [them]. *{Bad stuff is RED.}*

Psa 116:13 I will take the **cup of salvation**, and call upon the name of the LORD.

Isa 51:17 Awake, awake, stand up, O Jerusalem, which hast drunk at the hand of the LORD the **cup of his fury**; thou hast drunken the dregs of the cup of trembling, [and] wrung [them] out.

Isa 51:22 Thus saith thy Lord the LORD, and thy God [that] pleadeth the cause of his people, Behold, I have taken out of thine hand the cup of trembling, [even] the dregs of the **cup of my fury**; thou shalt no more drink it again:

Jer 16:7 Neither shall [men] tear [themselves] for them in mourning, to comfort them for the dead; neither shall [men] give them the cup of consolation to drink for their father or for their mother.

<u>Jer 25:15</u> For thus saith the LORD God of Israel unto me; Take the wine **cup of this fury** at my hand, and cause all the nations, to whom I send thee, to drink it.

<u>Jer 25:17</u> Then took I the cup at the LORD'S hand, and made all the nations to drink, unto whom the LORD had sent me:

<u>Jer 25:28</u> And it shall be, if they refuse to take the cup at thine hand to drink, then shalt thou say unto them, Thus saith the LORD of hosts; Ye shall certainly drink.

<u>Jer 49:12</u> For thus saith the LORD; Behold, they whose judgment [was] not to drink of the cup have assuredly drunken; and [art] thou he [that] shall altogether go unpunished? thou shalt not go unpunished, but thou shalt surely drink [of it].

<u>Jer 51:7</u> Babylon [hath been] a golden cup in the LORD'S hand, that made all the earth drunken: the nations have drunken of her wine; therefore the nations are mad.

<u>Lam 4:21</u> Rejoice and be glad, O daughter of Edom, that dwellest in the land of Uz; the cup also shall pass through unto thee: thou shalt be drunken, and shalt make thyself naked.

<u>Eze 23:31</u> Thou hast walked in the way of thy sister; therefore will I give her cup into thine hand. <u>Eze 23:32</u> Thus saith the Lord GOD; Thou shalt drink of thy sister's cup deep and large: thou shalt be laughed to scorn and had in derision; it containeth much. <u>Eze 23:33</u> Thou shalt be **filled with drunkenness and sorrow, with the cup of astonishment and desolation**, with the cup of thy sister Samaria.

<u>Hab 2:16</u> Thou art filled with shame for glory: drink thou also, and let thy foreskin be uncovered: the **cup of the LORD'S right hand shall be turned unto thee**, and shameful spewing [shall be] on thy glory.

<u>Zec 12:2</u> Behold, I will make Jerusalem a **cup of trembling** unto all the people round about, when they shall be in the siege both against Judah [and] against Jerusalem.

<u>Mat 10:42</u> And whosoever shall give to drink unto one of these little ones a cup of cold [water] only in the name of a disciple, verily I say unto you, he shall in no wise lose his reward.

Mat 20:22 But Jesus answered and said, Ye know not what ye ask. Are ye able to drink of the cup that I shall drink of, and to be baptized with the baptism that I am baptized with? They say unto him, We are able. Mat 20:23 And he saith unto them, Ye shall drink indeed of my cup, and be baptized with the baptism that I am baptized with: but to sit on my right hand, and on my left, is not mine to give, but [it shall be given to them] for whom it is prepared of my Father.

Mat 23:25 Woe unto you, scribes and Pharisees, hypocrites! for ye make clean the outside of the cup and of the platter, but within they are **full of extortion and excess**. Mat 23:26 [Thou] blind Pharisee, cleanse first that [which is] within the cup and platter, that the outside of them may be clean also.

Mat 26:27 And he took the cup, and gave thanks, and gave [it] to them, saying, Drink ye all of it;

Mat 26:39 And he went a little further, and fell on his face, and prayed, saying, O my Father, if it be possible, let this cup pass from me: nevertheless not as I will, but as thou [wilt].

Mat 26:42 He went away again the second time, and prayed, saying, O my Father, if this cup may not pass away from me, except I drink it, thy will be done.

Mar 9:41 For whosoever shall give you a cup of water to drink in my name, because ye belong to Christ, verily I say unto you, he shall not lose his reward.

Mar 10:38 But Jesus said unto them, Ye know not what ye ask: can ye drink of the cup that I drink of? and be baptized with the baptism that I am baptized with? Mar 10:39 And they said unto him, We can. And Jesus said unto them, Ye shall indeed drink of the cup that I drink of; and with the baptism that I am baptized withal shall ye be baptized:

Mar 14:23 And he took the cup, and when he had given thanks, he gave [it] to them: and they all drank of it.

Mar 14:36 And he said, Abba, Father, all things [are] possible unto thee; take away this cup from me: nevertheless not what I will, but what thou wilt.

<u>Luk 11:39</u> And the Lord said unto him, Now do ye Pharisees make clean the outside of the cup and the platter; but your inward part is full of ravening and wickedness.

<u>Luk 22:17</u> And he took the cup, and gave thanks, and said, Take this, and divide [it] among yourselves:

<u>Luk 22:20</u> Likewise also the cup after supper, saying, This **cup [is] the new testament in my blood**, which is shed for you.

<u>Luk 22:42</u> Saying, Father, if thou be willing, remove this cup from me: nevertheless not my will, but thine, be done.

<u>Jhn 18:11</u> Then said Jesus unto Peter, Put up thy sword into the sheath: the cup which my Father hath given me, shall I not drink it?

<u>1Cr 10:16</u> The **cup of blessing** which we bless, is it not the communion of the blood of Christ? The bread which we break, is it not the communion of the body of Christ?

<u>1Cr 10:21</u> Ye cannot drink the **cup of the Lord, and the cup of devils**: ye cannot be partakers of the Lord's table, and of the table of devils.

<u>1Cr 11:25</u> After the same manner also [he took] the cup, when he had supped, saying, This **cup is the new testament in my blood**: this do ye, as oft as ye drink [it], in remembrance of me. <u>1Cr 11:26</u> For as often as ye eat this bread, and drink this cup, ye do shew the Lord's death till he come. <u>1Cr 11:27</u> Wherefore whosoever shall eat this bread, and drink [this] cup of the Lord, unworthily, shall be guilty of the body and blood of the Lord. <u>1Cr 11:28</u> But let a man examine himself, and so let him eat of [that] bread, and drink of [that] cup.

<u>Rev 14:10</u> The same shall drink of the wine of the wrath of God, which is poured out without mixture into the **cup of his indignation**; and he shall be tormented with fire and brimstone in the presence of the holy angels, and in the presence of the Lamb:

<u>Rev 16:19</u> And the great city was divided into three parts, and the cities of the nations fell: and great Babylon came in remembrance before God, to give unto her the **cup of the wine of the fierceness of his wrath**.

Rev 17:4 And the woman was arrayed in purple and scarlet colour, and decked with gold and precious stones and pearls, having a golden **cup in her hand full of abominations and filthiness of her fornication**:

Rev 18:6 Reward her even as she rewarded you, and double unto her double according to her works: in the **cup which she hath filled fill to her double**.

CUPS

Isa 22:24 And they shall hang upon him all the glory of his father's house, the offspring and the issue, all **vessels of small quantity, from the vessels of cups, even to all the vessels of flagons.** *{different sizes}*

Jer 35:5 And I set before the sons of the house of the Rechabites pots full of wine, and cups, and I said unto them, Drink ye wine.

Mar 7:8 For laying aside the commandment of God, ye hold the tradition of men, [as] the washing of pots and cups: and many other such like things ye do.

VESSEL

Psa 2:9 Thou shalt break them with a rod of iron; thou shalt dash them in pieces like a potter's vessel.

Psa 31:12 I am forgotten as a dead man out of mind: I am like a broken vessel.

Pro 25:4 Take away the dross from the silver, and there shall come forth a vessel for the finer. *{holiness}*

Isa 30:14 And he shall break it as the breaking of the potters' vessel that is broken in pieces; he shall not spare: so that there shall not be found in the bursting of it a sherd to take fire from the hearth, or to take water [withal] out of the pit.

Jer 18:4 And the vessel that he made of clay was marred in the hand of the potter: so he made it again another vessel, as seemed good to the potter to make [it].

Jer 19:11 And shalt say unto them, Thus saith the LORD of hosts; Even so will I break this people and this city, as [one] breaketh a potter's vessel, that cannot be made whole again: and they shall bury [them] in Tophet, till [there be] no place to bury.

Jer 48:11 Moab hath been at ease from his youth, and he hath settled on his lees, and hath **not been emptied from vessel to vessel**, neither hath he gone into captivity: therefore his taste remained in him, and his scent is not changed.

Jer 48:38 [There shall be] lamentation generally upon all the housetops of Moab, and in the streets thereof: for I have broken Moab like a **vessel wherein [is] no pleasure**, saith the LORD.

Jer 51:34 Nebuchadrezzar the king of Babylon hath devoured me, he hath crushed me, he hath made me an empty vessel, he hath swallowed me up like a dragon, he hath filled his belly with my delicates, he hath cast me out.

Hsa 8:8 Israel is swallowed up: now shall they be among the Gentiles as a **vessel wherein [is] no pleasure**.

Act 9:15 But the Lord said unto him, Go thy way: for he is a **chosen vessel** unto me, to bear my name before the Gentiles, and kings, and the children of Israel:

Rom 9:21 Hath not the potter power over the clay, of the same lump to make one **vessel unto honour, and another unto dishonour**? {different levels or uses or values}

1Th 4:4 That every one of you should know how to possess his **vessel in sanctification and honour**;

2Ti 2:21 If a man therefore purge himself from these, he shall be a **vessel unto honour**, sanctified, and meet for the master's use, [and] prepared unto every good work.

1Pe 3:7 Likewise, ye husbands, dwell with [them] according to knowledge, giving honour unto the wife, as unto **the weaker vessel**, and as being heirs together of the grace of life; that your prayers be not hindered.

VESSELS

Exd 40:9 And thou shalt take the anointing oil, and anoint the tabernacle, and all that [is] therein, and shalt hallow it, and all the vessels thereof: and it shall be holy. Exd 40:9 And thou shalt take the anointing oil, and anoint the tabernacle, and all that [is] therein, and shalt hallow it, and all the vessels thereof: and it shall be holy.

2Ch 36:18 And all the vessels of the house of God, great and small, and the treasures of the house of the LORD, and the treasures of the king, and of his princes; all [these] he brought to Babylon.

2Ch 36:19 And they burnt the house of God, and brake down the wall of Jerusalem, and burnt all the palaces thereof with fire, and destroyed all the goodly vessels thereof.

Ezr 5:14 And the vessels also of gold and silver of the house of God, which Nebuchadnezzar took out of the temple that [was] in Jerusalem, and brought them into the temple of Babylon, those did Cyrus the king take out of the temple of Babylon, and they were delivered unto [one], whose name [was] Sheshbazzar, whom he had made governor; Ezr 5:15 And said unto him, Take these vessels, go, carry them into the temple that [is] in Jerusalem, and let the house of God be builded in his place.

Ezr 7:19 The vessels also that are given thee for the service of the house of thy God, [those] deliver thou before the God of Jerusalem.

Isa 22:24 And they shall hang upon him all the glory of his father's house, the offspring and the issue, all **vessels of small quantity, from the vessels of cups, even to all the vessels of flagons**.

Isa 52:11 Depart ye, depart ye, go ye out from thence, touch no unclean [thing]; go ye out of the midst of her; be ye clean, that bear the vessels of the LORD.

Isa 65:4 Which remain among the graves, and lodge in the monuments, which eat swine's flesh, and broth of **abominable [things is in] their vessels**;

Jer 28:3 Within two full years will I bring again into this place all the vessels of the LORD'S house, that Nebuchadnezzar king of Babylon took away from this place, and carried them to Babylon:

Jer 28:6 Even the prophet Jeremiah said, Amen: the LORD do so: the LORD perform thy words which thou hast prophesied, to bring again the vessels of the LORD'S house, and all that is carried away captive, from Babylon into this place.

Jer 48:12 Therefore, behold, the days come, saith the LORD, that I will send unto him wanderers, that shall cause him to wander, and shall empty his vessels, and break their bottles.

Mat 13:48 Which, when it was full, they drew to shore, and sat down, and gathered the good into vessels, but cast the bad away.

Mat 25:4 But the wise took oil in their vessels with their lamps.

Rom 9:22 [What] if God, willing to shew [his] wrath, and to make his power known, endured with much longsuffering the **vessels of wrath** fitted to destruction: Rom 9:23 And that he might make known the riches of his glory on the vessels of mercy, which he had afore prepared unto glory,

2Cr 4:7 But we have this treasure in **earthen vessels**, that the excellency of the power may be of God, and not of us.

2Ti 2:20 But in a great house there are not only vessels of gold and of silver, but also of wood and of earth; and some to honour, and some to dishonour. {noble and ignoble}

Rev 2:27 And he shall rule them with a rod of iron; as the vessels of a potter shall they be broken to shivers: even as I received of my Father.

BOTTLE / BOTTLES (WINESKIN/S)

Psa 119:83 For I am become like a bottle in the smoke; [yet] do I not forget thy statutes.

Jer 13:12 Therefore thou shalt speak unto them this word; Thus saith the LORD God of Israel, Every bottle shall be filled with wine: and they shall say unto thee, Do we not certainly know that every bottle shall be filled with wine? 13 Then shalt thou say unto them, Thus saith the LORD, Behold, I will fill all the inhabitants of this land, even the kings that sit upon David's throne, and the priests, and the prophets, and all the inhabitants of Jerusalem, with drunkenness.

Job 38:37 Who can number the clouds in wisdom? or who can stay the **bottles of heaven**,

Jer 48:12 Therefore, behold, the days come, saith the LORD, that I will send unto him wanderers, that shall cause him to wander, and shall **empty his vessels, and break their bottles**.

Mat 9:17 Neither do men put new wine into old bottles: else the bottles break, and the wine runneth out, and the bottles perish: but they put new wine into new bottles, and both are preserved.

Mar 2:22 And no man putteth new wine into old bottles: else the new wine doth burst the bottles, and the wine is spilled, and the bottles will be marred: but new wine must be put into new bottles.

Luk 5:37 And no man putteth new wine into old bottles; else the new wine will burst the bottles, and be spilled, and the bottles shall perish.

Luk 5:38 But new wine must be put into new bottles; and both are preserved.

CISTERN(S)

2Ki 18:31 Hearken not to Hezekiah: for thus saith the king of Assyria, Make [an agreement] with me by a present, and come out to me, and [then] eat ye every man of his own vine, and every one of his fig tree, and drink ye every one the waters of his cistern:

Pro 5:15 Drink waters out of thine own cistern, and running waters out of thine own well.

Ecc 12:6 Or ever the silver cord be loosed, or the golden bowl be broken, or the pitcher be broken at the fountain, or the wheel broken at the cistern.

Jer 2:13 For my people have committed two evils; they have forsaken me the fountain of living waters, [and] hewed them out cisterns, broken cisterns, that can hold no water. *{tried to fill their own cups from their own reservoirs}*

BOWL

<u>Ecc 12:6</u> Or ever the silver cord be loosed, or the golden bowl be broken, or the pitcher be broken at the fountain, or the wheel broken at the cistern.

<u>Zec 4:2</u> And said unto me, What seest thou? And I said, I have looked, and behold a candlestick all [of] gold, with a bowl upon the top of it, and his seven lamps thereon, and seven pipes to the seven lamps, which [are] upon the top thereof:

<u>Zec 4:3</u> And two olive trees by it, one upon the right [side] of the bowl, and the other upon the left [side] thereof.

BOWLS

<u>Num 7:84</u> This [was] the dedication of the altar, in the day when it was anointed, by the princes of Israel: twelve chargers of silver, twelve silver bowls, twelve spoons of gold:

<u>Zec 9:15</u> The LORD of hosts shall defend them; and they shall devour, and subdue with sling stones; and they shall drink, [and] make a noise as through wine; and they shall be filled like bowls, [and] as the corners of the altar.

<u>Zec 14:20</u> In that day shall there be upon the bells of the horses, HOLINESS UNTO THE LORD; and the pots in the LORD'S house shall be like the bowls before the altar.

OVERFLOW

<u>Isa 10:22</u> For though thy people Israel be as the sand of the sea, [yet] a remnant of them shall return: the consumption decreed shall overflow with righteousness.

<u>Joe 2:24</u> And the floors shall be full of wheat, and the fats shall overflow with wine and oil.

<u>Joe 3:13</u> Put ye in the sickle, for the harvest is ripe: come, get you down; for the press is full, the **fats overflow; for their wickedness [is] great**. *{that would be vats in regular English}*

POT

2Ki 4:2 And Elisha said unto her, What shall I do for thee? tell me, what hast thou in the house? And she said, Thine handmaid hath not any thing in the house, save a pot of oil.

Job 41:31 He maketh the deep to boil like a pot: he maketh the sea like a pot of ointment

Pro 17:3 The fining pot [is] for silver, and the furnace for gold: but the LORD trieth the hearts.

Pro 27:21 [As] the fining pot for silver, and the furnace for gold; so [is] a man to his praise.

Ecc 7:6 For as the crackling of thorns under a pot, so [is] the laughter of the fool: this also [is] vanity.

Jer 1:13 And the word of the LORD came unto me the second time, saying, What seest thou? And I said, I see a seething pot; and the face thereof [is] toward the north.

Eze 24:3 And utter a parable unto the rebellious house, and say unto them, Thus saith the Lord GOD; Set on a pot, set [it] on, and also pour water into it: {pot used as parable}

Eze 24:6 Wherefore thus saith the Lord GOD; Woe to the bloody city, to the **pot whose scum [is] therein**, and whose scum is not gone out of it! bring it out piece by piece; let no lot fall upon it.

Mic 3:3 Who also eat the flesh of my people, and flay their skin from off them; and they break their bones, and chop them in pieces, as for the pot, and as flesh within the caldron.

Zec 14:21 Yea, **every pot in Jerusalem and in Judah shall be holiness** unto the LORD of hosts: and all they that sacrifice shall come and take of them, and seethe therein: and in that day there shall be no more the Canaanite in the house of the LORD of hosts.

Hbr 9:4 Which had the golden censer, and the ark of the covenant overlaid round about with gold, wherein [was] the golden pot that had manna, and Aaron's rod that budded, and the tables of the covenant;

POTS

<u>Lev 11:35</u> And every [thing] whereupon [any part] of their carcase falleth shall be unclean; [whether it be] oven, or ranges for pots, they shall be broken down: [for] they [are] unclean, and shall be unclean unto you.

<u>Psa 58:9</u> Before your pots can feel the thorns, he shall take them away as with a whirlwind, both living, and in [his] wrath.

<u>Psa 68:13</u> Though ye have lien among the pots, [yet shall ye be as] the wings of a dove covered with silver, and her feathers with yellow gold.

<u>Psa 81:6</u> I removed his shoulder from the burden: his hands were delivered from the pots.

<u>Jer 35:5</u> And I set before the sons of the house of the Rechabites pots full of wine, and cups, and I said unto them, Drink ye wine.

<u>Zec 14:20</u> In that day shall there be upon the bells of the horses, HOLINESS UNTO THE LORD; and the pots in the LORD'S house shall be like the bowls before the altar.

<u>Mar 7:8</u> For laying aside the commandment of God, ye hold the tradition of men, [as] the washing of pots and cups: and many other such like things ye do.

DWELLETH

<u>Jhn 6:56</u> He that eateth my flesh, and drinketh my blood, **dwelleth in me, and I in him**. *{blue stuff}*

<u>Jhn 14:17</u> [Even] the Spirit of truth; whom the world cannot receive, because it seeth him not, neither knoweth him: but ye know him; for he **dwelleth with you, and shall be in you**.

<u>Act 7:48</u> Howbeit the most High dwelleth not in temples made with hands; as saith the prophet,

<u>Act 17:24</u> God that made the world and all things therein, seeing that he is Lord of heaven and earth, dwelleth not in temples made with hands;

<u>Rom 7:17</u> Now then it is no more I that do it, but **sin that dwelleth in me**. *{red stuff}*

Rom 7:18 For I know that in me (that is, in my flesh,) dwelleth no good thing: for to will is present with me; but [how] to perform that which is good I find not. *{yellow stuff}*

Rom 7:20 Now if I do that I would not, it is no more I that do it, but sin that dwelleth in me.

1Cr 3:16 Know ye not that ye are the temple of God, and [that] the **Spirit of God dwelleth in you**?

Col 2:9 For in him dwelleth all the fulness of the Godhead bodily.

2Ti 1:14 That good thing which was committed unto thee keep by the **Holy Ghost which dwelleth in us**.

Jam 4:5 Do ye think that the scripture saith in vain, The **spirit that dwelleth in us** lusteth to envy?

1Jo 3:24 And he that keepeth his commandments **dwelleth in him, and he in him**. And hereby we know that he abideth in us, by the Spirit which he hath given us.

1Jo 4:12 No man hath seen God at any time. If we love one another, **God dwelleth in us**, and his love is perfected in us.

1Jo 4:15 Whosoever shall confess that Jesus is the Son of God, **God dwelleth in him, and he in God**.

1Jo 4:16 And we have known and believed the love that God hath to us. God is love; and he that **dwelleth in love dwelleth in God, and God in him**.

2Jo 1:2 For the truth's sake, which **dwelleth in us**, and shall be with us for ever.

VATS

Joel 2:24 – The threshing floors will be filled with grain; the vats will overflow with new wine and oil.

Joe 3:13 Put ye in the sickle, for the harvest is ripe: come, get you down; for the press is full, the vats overflow; for their wickedness [is] great.

APPENDIX C
PIECES THAT WERE LEFT OVER AFTER
WE PUT THE BICYCLE TOGETHER

Col 1:27 To whom God would make known what [is] the riches of the glory of this mystery among the Gentiles; which is **Christ in you**, the hope of glory:

2Cr 13:5 Examine yourselves, whether ye be in the faith; prove your own selves. Know ye not your own selves, how that **Jesus Christ is in you**, except ye be reprobates?

Gal 4:19 My little children, of whom I travail in birth again until Christ be formed in you,

Phm 1:6 That the communication of thy faith may become effectual by the acknowledging of every good thing which is in you in Christ Jesus.

Foolish Rich Man – Built barns and stored wealth, got stagnant and God killed him. State of the Church.

<u>Prov. 10:11</u> – The mouth of a righteous [man is] a **well of life**: but violence covereth the mouth of the wicked.

<u>Prov. 25:26</u> – A righteous man falling down before the wicked [is as] a **troubled fountain, and a corrupt spring**.

<u>Song of Solomon 4:9-15</u> -You have stolen my heart, my sister, my bride; you have stolen my heart with one glance of your eyes, with one jewel of your necklace. How delightful is your love, my sister, my bride! How much more pleasing is your love than wine, and the fragrance of your perfume than any spice! Your lips drop sweetness as the honeycomb, my bride; milk and honey are under your tongue. The fragrance of your garments is like that of Lebanon. You are a **garden locked up**, my sister, my bride; you are a **spring enclosed, a sealed fountain.** Your plants are an orchard of pomegranates with choice fruits, with henna and nard, nard and saffron, calamus and cinnamon, with every kind of incense tree, with myrrh and aloes and all the finest spices. You are a garden fountain, a well of flowing water streaming down from Lebanon.

<u>Isaiah 12:1-6</u> – 1 In that day you will say: "I will praise you, O LORD. Although you were angry with me, your anger has turned away and you have comforted me. 2 Surely God is my salvation; I will trust and not be afraid. The LORD, the LORD, is my strength and my song; he has become my salvation." 3 With joy you will **draw water from the wells of salvation**. 4 In that day you will say: "Give thanks to the LORD, call on his name; make known among the nations what he has done, and proclaim that his name is exalted. 5 Sing to the LORD, for he has done glorious things; let this be known to all the world. 6 Shout aloud and sing for joy, people of Zion, for great is the Holy One of Israel among you."

<u>Hosea 13:15</u> – Though he be fruitful among [his] brethren, an east wind shall come, the wind of the LORD shall come up from the wilderness, and **his spring shall become dry, and his fountain shall be dried up:** he shall spoil the treasure of all pleasant vessels

<u>Isaiah 41:17</u> – [When] the poor and needy seek water, and [there is] none, [and] their tongue faileth for **thirst, I the LORD will hear them, I the God of Israel will not forsake them**.

<u>Isaiah 41:18</u> – I will open rivers in high places, and fountains in the midst of the valleys: I will make the wilderness a pool of water, and the dry land springs of water.

<u>Isaiah 41:19</u> – I will plant in the wilderness the cedar, the shittah tree, and the myrtle, and the oil tree; I will set in the desert the fir tree, [and] the pine, and the box tree together:

<u>Isaiah 41:20</u> – That they may see, and know, and consider, and understand together, that the hand of the LORD hath done this, and the Holy One of Israel hath created it.

{People will flourish in places where there should be no water. They will be out in the wilderness and yet they will thrive. Trees that should NOT grow in the desert will flourish. People will be outside of "church" and yet they will have great big cups full of Jesus. }

<u>Rom 8:9</u> But ye are not in the flesh, but in the Spirit, if so be that the Spirit of God dwell in you. Now if any man have not the Spirit of Christ, he is none of his.

<u>Rom 8:10</u> And if Christ [be] in you, the body [is] dead because of sin; but the Spirit [is] life because of righteousness.

Rom 8:11 But if the Spirit of him that raised up Jesus from the dead dwell in you, he that raised up Christ from the dead shall also quicken your mortal bodies by his Spirit that dwelleth in you.

Hosea 13:15 – Though he be fruitful among [his] brethren, an east wind shall come, the wind of the LORD shall come up from the wilderness, and his spring shall become dry, and his fountain shall be dried up: he shall spoil the treasure of all pleasant vessels.

Hosea 13:15 (NIV) – even though he thrives among his brothers. An east wind from the LORD will come, blowing in from the desert; his spring will fail and his well dry up. His storehouse will be plundered of all its treasures.

{If the Lord wants to, He will suck all the good stuff out of your cup and you will be dry. Then your jar of clay will crack and spoil, no matter how pleasant you think it is. }

John 4:14 But whosoever drinketh of the water that I shall give him shall never thirst; but the water that I shall give him shall be in him a well of water springing up into everlasting life.

John 4:23:24 But the hour cometh, and now is, when the true worshipers shall worship the Father in spirit and in truth: for the Father seeketh such to worship him. God [is] a Spirit: and they that worship him must worship [him] in spirit and in truth.

Not in mind and body. IN SPIRIT which is the only place true TRUTH can come from.

<u>2 Peter 2:9-22</u> The Lord knoweth how to deliver the godly out of temptations, and to reserve the unjust unto the day of judgment to be punished: But chiefly them that walk after the flesh in the lust of uncleanness, and despise government. Presumptuous [are they], selfwilled, they are not afraid to speak evil of dignities. Whereas angels, which are greater in power and might, bring not railing accusation against them before the Lord. But these, as natural brute beasts, made to be taken and destroyed, speak evil of the things that they understand not; and shall utterly perish in their own corruption; And shall receive the reward of unrighteousness, [as] they that count it pleasure to riot in the day time. Spots [they are] and blemishes, sporting themselves with their own deceivings while they feast with you; Having eyes full of adultery, and that cannot cease from sin; beguiling unstable souls: an heart they have exercised with covetous practices; cursed children: Which have forsaken the right way, and are gone astray, following the way of Balaam [the son] of Bosor, who loved the wages of unrighteousness; But was rebuked for his iniquity: the dumb ass speaking with man's voice forbad the madness of the prophet. These are wells without water, clouds that are carried with a tempest; to whom the mist of darkness is reserved for ever. For when they speak great swelling [words] of vanity, they allure through the lusts of the flesh, [through much] wantonness, those that were clean escaped from them who live in error. While they promise them **liberty**, they themselves are the servants of corruption: for of whom a man is overcome, of the same is he brought in bondage. For if after they have escaped the pollutions of the world through the knowledge of the Lord and Saviour Jesus Christ, they are again entangled therein, and overcome, the latter end is worse with them than the beginning. For it had

been better for them not to have known the way of righteousness, than, after they have known [it], to turn from the holy commandment delivered unto them. But it is happened unto them according to the true proverb, The dog [is] turned to his own vomit again; and the sow that was washed to her wallowing in the mire.

Revelation 7:17 – For the Lamb which is in the midst of the throne shall feed them, and shall lead them unto **living fountains of waters**: and God shall wipe away all tears from their eyes.

There is also something really cool in Mark 12 about the parable of the tenants. The Landowner buys a piece of land - as God purchased all of us through Christ - even the unsaved are His, the enemy had to give up all his territory. Then the Landowner builds a wall around it - as God puts a hedge around us against the enemy. Then he dug a vat for the winepress - as God give us all a "cup". Then he built a watchtower - as God gives us conscience to keep guard. THEN he rents it all back to some tenants, on the condition that he get the first fruits and they respond appropriately to the commitment they made with Him. It's HIS land and they need to acknowledge it and act like it. When he comes to collect, they beat and kill his messengers. If they refuse to receive His Son, then He will come in and kill them and give all they possessed to another. If the Son stands at the door and knocks and they refuse to respond, then they will die. If they had Kingdom responsibilities and potential Kingdom treasure, it will be given to another to fulfill and benefit from. The bad tenants filled their vat with the wrong stuff.

APPENDIX D
OPEN LETTER OF APOLOGY TO THE WORLD

Please bear with me, this is long overdue and there's lots of ground to cover. I want to make sure that I get it all out. Not just for me, but because I think you need to hear it. Maybe there are other Christians out there as well that need to make apologies and will find courage here. I appreciate your time, I know it's valuable.

Dear Members of the World,

I'm just a guy, nobody really. Son of a preacher and missionary. Years and years of Vacation Bible Schools, summer camps, youth ski trips, puppet shows, revivals, choir trips - you name it. Even went to a Christian college and got a degree in religion. I ended up in the business world, but I spent two decades tithing, sitting on committees, teaching Sunday School, going to seminars and conferences, etc. I even met my wife in the single's class at church. I'm not a bad guy, I've been mostly behaving myself and everybody seems to like me. I do some good stuff here and there.

But lately I've been trying to understand Jesus more and stuff I never noticed before has really started to bug me. I've been taking a look around and I'm having a hard time making sense of what it is we've built here. So, it just seemed like, whether anybody else says it or not, I need to take responsibility for the part I played and say what I have to say.

Here we go ...

I know you think that Christians are a big bunch of hypocrites. We say we're more "religious" and we're going to heaven and you're not, and then we drive our big shiny cars with little fishies on the trunk and cut you off in traffic as we race by the homeless guy on the corner. We average just 2% of our money to church and charity, despite that we say the Bible is the word of God and **it** says we're supposed to give **everything**. On average, we buy just as many big screen TVs and bass boats and fur coats and makeup and baseball cards and online porn as anybody else. Maybe more. You've seen leader after leader end up in jail or court or a sex scandal of one sort or another.

Well ... you're right. We're guilty of all of it. We've done it all. And, I'm really sorry.

You see our cheesy TV shows and slick guys begging for money and you get that there's something seriously sneaky and wrong here. A high-pressure call for money so they can stay on the air? Were we supposed to use Jesus as just another form of entertainment? Who do we think we're kidding? Where's Jesus in all this? Aren't we supposed to rely on him? Isn't He going to meet our needs if we're inside His will?

What happened to sacrifice and suffering and helping the poor? I'm just sick about this. I mean, the church leaders, they're not all bad guys, there are lots and lots of really hard-working well-meaning folks who love and care and are meeting real needs in the community. Some of them understand and love Jesus - but I'm just real sure <u>those</u> pastors don't drive Bentley's, have multi-million dollar homes and their own lear jets! I mean, what "god" are we worshipping? Money? Ego? Power?

You see our massive shiny new buildings all over the place. Heck, maybe we even kicked you out of your house so we could expand our parking lots. You can't figure out why we need four different Christian churches on four corners of the same intersection. We've got playgrounds and bowling alleys and basketball leagues. We've got Starbucks coffee in the sanctuary. We've got orchestras and giant chandeliers and fountains out front. We've got bookstores full of "jesus junk" with every imaginable style and flavor of religious knick-knack. But where's Jesus? Is this what HE wanted?

Oh, sure, there are good folks all over and not every church is such a mess, but Christians are the ones that say we're supposed to be "One Body." So even the good ones are guilty of not putting a stop to it sooner. We were supposed to keep each other in line and not tolerate factions and dissensions and greed and idolatry and all this other bad stuff. Man, we really blew it! We've got 33,000 denominations and most of them won't talk to the other ones. We lose over $5 million a day to fraud from "trusted" people inside the church! We spend 95% of all our money on our own comforts and programs and happy family fun time shows and we let 250 MILLION Christians in other countries live on the very edge of starvation. Not to mention the billion or so that have never even once heard of Jesus - or the homeless guy downtown we almost ran over when we cut you off.

We're as guilty as we can be. All of us. Nobody is exempt. We should have put a stop to it a lot sooner. But I can't apologize on behalf of anyone else. This is about me.

I know that you might have gone to church as a kid and stopped going as soon as you could. I know that you might even have been abused by somebody in the church! Maybe we got you all fired up and then just let you drift off like we didn't really care. Maybe you just don't fit our "profile." You might have piercings and purple hair or tattoos or been in jail -- and somewhere inside you just know that even if you wanted to go to church one Sunday, it would not go well. I'm sorry for that. Jesus loves you. He always hung out with the most unexpected people. He had the biggest heart for the folks everybody else tried to ignore. What have we done? We've told you to put on a sweater and some loafers or you can't go to heaven. I just want to throw up.

Look, I know you're mad. And you have a right to be. We've done you wrong for a LONG time now. There's some things about Jesus that people need to hear, but we've buried a beautiful masterpiece under hundreds of layers of soft pink latex paint. If you have a Bible handy, look up Matthew 23. (If you don't, you can look it up here - www.BibleGateway.com .) Find it? Read it carefully, the Pharisees were the "religious" people of the day, the leaders of the faith. In this chapter Jesus SEVEN times says how pitiful and wretched and cursed they are for what they're doing to the people they're supposed to be leading. He even calls them "white washed tombs of dead mens bones" and a "brood of vipers"! I don't have time here, but read it and see if we're not doing EVERY single one of those things. Jesus can't possibly be happy about what we've done to you.

Sure, we like to kid ourselves and pretend everything is OK - but it's not. We're hated. Now, please understand, Jesus was hated, too. But that was because he said hard things and sometimes people don't like hearing the Truth. And he promised we would be hated if we were like him. But that's not why we're hated at the moment. We're hated right now because we're a giant pack of lying hypocrites that say one thing and do something else altogether. If we were hated because we were like Jesus, that would be one thing, but that's not it at all. You see right through our happy music and fluffy services and you can tell there's something desperately wrong here. We're no different than anybody else - except that we say we're better than you.

It was never supposed to be like this. Jesus asked us to care for the widows and orphans, to feed the hungry, care for the sick, visit those in prison, reach the lost. He wanted us to love our enemies and pray for them. He cared about human justice and suffering, the lost and lonely. But I don't think He would have marched on a picket line - He had His mind on much bigger problems. He wanted us to focus on the eternal things, not the everyday. He never once said to go into all the world and build big buildings and divide up into factions and buy Bentleys. Just the opposite! I get that you're mad at us and I think you have a right to be, but please understand, you're mad at what we've made under our own power, you're mad at "Churchianity." That's different than Christ and what he wanted. Don't be mad at Jesus! This mess wasn't His idea!

Look, I'm really sorry. I accept responsibility for my part in having hurt you. But I'm committing to you all, dear Members of the World, that I'm not going to do it any more. Not a single penny more. I'm not going to put my faith in "Churchianity" or any leader or program or TV show -- but in Christ Jesus and His salvation. That's when I was set free and began to see that God wants and expects more of us than this. And I'm not helping anybody that's not fully committed to the same thing.

It took centuries to build this monster, so it's not like it's going to just turn around overnight. But the times are changing and we're way overdue for something new. Big bad things are happening - like the tsunami in Asia - and I think more are coming. I don't want any more time to go by without having said this. I'm sorry for all the time and money I've wasted. But Jesus saves. Really. The church itself isn't even the point. Jesus is the real deal. He lived and He died for my sins and He rose again. He is who He said He was and He cares about me - and you. He's our only hope. We need places you can go that will only teach Jesus and will not be swayed or tempted or distracted by anything else. God willing, that's coming.

Please don't think all Christians are just posers. Some of them really mean it when they say they belong to Christ. The problem is mostly in the West where we're all comfy and complacent and seem to like it that way. The Christians in China and other places are deadly serious. There's no room for anything but Jesus when you're on the run from the government. They are dying every day for their faith and doing crazy hard things because they're absolutely committed to Christ. These are martyrs. People willing to crucify little pieces of themselves every day to be more like Christ. People willing to set aside everything they want to do what Christ wants. People willing to rot in prison or take a beating or die if that's what it's going to take. People that act in pure love and never back down. I'm not worthy to tie their shoes. And there are some like that here, too, and I hope we can get a lot more people to start living that way. It's way overdue.

If you're talking to someone and they tell you they're a Christian, ask them if they're the kind of Christian that really means it all the time or the kind that just means it on Sunday. The Bible says we'll know them by their "fruits" - by the faith and purity and love in their deeds and words. When you find one that proves Christ is in them by how much they love you, ask them to tell you all about Jesus. If you know one of those fearless martyrs that speaks nothing but pure, clean, hard Truth - ask lots of questions. Truth is a lot more rare than you would think. But don't settle for soft, fluffy and comfortable anymore - that's not in the Bible.

As for me and my house, we're really sorry. From now on, we're going to serve the Lord, not "Churchianity." We're going to try to call together as many of those martyrs as we can and start doing what Christ wanted. If I run into you someday, please give me a chance to shake your hand and apologize in person. I'm going to try harder from now on, I promise. I think there are lots of others feeling the same way, so don't be surprised if you start hearing stuff like this more often.

Thanks for your time. I hope it helps.

Doug Perry - Liberty, Missouri, USA
www.FellowshipOfTheMartyrs.com
fotm@FellowshipOfTheMartyrs.com

ABOUT THE AUTHOR

Doug Perry has been going 200 miles an hour with his hair on fire since November 23, 2004 when God showed him an open vision of how much God loves His children, how angry God is for how we're killing His children, and how much we have to hurry. It's safe to say that praying to see through the eyes of Jesus and be dangerous to satan wrecked his life. He had a nice home, a wife, two kids, two dogs, a foreign car with a sunroof, and a multimillion dollar, award-winning business that was named the #4 fastest growing company in Kansas City in 2006. Shoot, he was even teaching Sunday School.

Then he realized what he was, what we've built, and how it looks in the light of holiness. He realized he was a friend of the world – and an enemy of God. (James 4:4) So he sold all he had and gave it to the poor – or it was stripped from him one way or another.

And it was all worth it.

Now he's the author of seven books, nearly a thousand videos, music, poetry, and founder of a homeless shelter and a food pantry that feeds 5,000+ people every month. He has cried on the sidewalk in public for days. He's been arrested on false charges. He's spent weeks at a time in prayer, fasting and weeping for the sad state of things.

And he's been spit on, lied about, abandoned, forsaken by friends, banned by pastors, ejected from sanctuaries – and looks more like Jesus all the time. He's even had people try to physically kill him! Just for speaking the hard truth nobody wants to hear. But Jesus said it would be like that. Praise God! Bring it on.
If nobody is shooting at you, then you're not dangerous.

Statistics about the church are from:

World Christian Trends, Ad 30-Ad 2200: Interpreting the Annual Christian Megacensus, by David B. Barrett & Todd M. Johnson, William Carey Library Pub.

Also quotes from **"The Normal Christian Church Life"** by Watchman Nee.

Bible verses are quoted from: KJV, NIV, Darby, Wycliffe or Young's (and one from The Message).

Rights belong to their respective owners or trademark holders or patent registers or whatever they are.

I didn't ask for permission to quote from them.

I suspect some of them don't like what I'm saying and wouldn't endorse it. Just so you know. ;-)

OTHER TITLES FROM
FELLOWSHIP OF THE MARTYRS
PUBLISHING

Rain Right NOW, Lord! - from Doug Perry
What is it going to take for God to pour His Spirit out on all flesh? Or is He waiting for us? Are spiritual gifts real and for today – and how do you get more of them?

The Apology to the World – from Doug Perry
The "Apology to the World" letter has influenced thousands and been all over the world. This book spawned from responses to that letter and collected writings about the need for change.

Left-Handed Warriors – from Linda Carriger
A suspenseful tale of the supernatural vs. the natural. What was it like for kids growing up in the book of Acts? Linda paints a picture of what it's like to be radically sold out to Christ – and still a kid.

Missionaries are Human, Too – from Nancy Perry
A sweet, candid look at what it's like to be a missionary family learning to trust God in a foreign country. Written in 1976.

Dialogues With God – from Doug Perry
Some discussions between Doug and the Almighty, along with a trouble-shooting guide to help you get unclogged, get your cup full and hear God better.

DEMONS?! You're kidding, right? - from Doug Perry
A very detailed guide to spiritual warfare – how the bad guys act, what they look like, where they hide and much more. For experts only. Not for sissies. Seriously. We're not kidding.

Do It Yourself City Church Restoration – from Doug Perry
What was 'church' supposed to be like all along? Are we doing it right? What's it going to take to fix it? If Jesus Christ wrote a letter to the Body of Christ in your city, could you bear to read it? What would happen if you were One Body in your town?

Who Neutered the Holy Spirit?! - from Doug Perry

Why do people say that the Holy Spirit stopped doing all the cool stuff that used to happen? This details the scriptural evidence of the work of the Spirit in the Old Testament, in the New Testament, after Pentecost, and in the church today. Along with help to get you unclogged so you can walk in the fullness of what God has for you.

The Red Dragon: the horrifying truth about why the 'church' cannot seem to change – from Doug Perry

How bad are things? How did they get this bad? In fact, they're SO bad, they have to be considered supernaturally bad! In fact, it's a curse from God. A delusion sent on those that went their own way. Weep. No really, weep! That's your only hope.

Expelling Xavier – from Dorothy Haile

A love story between a girl possessed by something dark and a boy just learning who he is in Christ – and their Savior. A very different kind of Christian novel, gritty, rough and fiercely transparent about the realities of life under the control of the darkness.

The Big Picture Book – from Doug Perry

Coming soon. Answers to some of the DEEP questions.

Fellowship Of The Martyrs Volume 1 – from Doug Perry

One mega book combining:
> The Apology to the World
> The Red Dragon
> Dialogues with God
> Rain Right NOW, Lord!
> Do It Yourself City Church Restoration

A compete course; from what's wrong with the church, how to fix YOU first, how to get your cup full and get big and strong and then how to bring real revival and restore the manifestation of "church" in your town as it was always meant to be.

**And LOTS more titles coming soon!!
And in SPANISH!**

Made in the USA
Columbia, SC
03 February 2025

52593326R00152